simply
Baking

p

This is a Parragon Publishing book
First published in 2001

Parragon Publishing
Queen Street House
4 Queen Street
Bath, BA1 1HE, UK

ISBN: 1-84273-216-1

Printed in China

Produced by The Bridgewater Book Company Ltd.

Art Director: Stephen Knowlden
Editorial Director: Fiona Biggs
Senior Editor: Mark Truman
Editorial Assistant: Tom Kitch
Photography: St John Asprey
Home Economist: Jacqueline Bellefontaine

NOTE
Tablespoons are assumed to be 15 ml.
Unless otherwise stated, milk is assumed
to be whole fat, eggs are medium and pepper
is freshly ground black pepper.

contents

introduction

This beautifully illustrated book brings you all the skills you need to recreate some of the best-loved traditional baking dishes. It also shows you how to experiment with some of the exciting contemporary ingredients now readily available in leading supermarkets. Clear step-by-step instructions guide you through the techniques needed to mastermind all those baking favorites that have been savored and enjoyed from generation to generation.

Breads & Savories

Making bread at home is great fun and allows you to experiment with all sorts of ingredients, such as sun-dried tomatoes, garlic, mangoes, and olive oil, to create versatile and delicious variations of modern breads, rolls, and loaves. Chapter 4 also shows you how to spice up all sorts of savories with exciting adaptations of traditional tarts, pies, and cookies, such as Curry Pasties, Creamy Red Onion & Asparagus Flan, Red Onion & Thyme Tart, and delicious Mini Celery Pies.

Vegetarian Cooking

Vegetarian recipes full of delicious wholesome ingredients, which are every bit as good as traditional baking favorites, have been created in Chapter 4. Recipes include Dairy-free Lentil, Onion & Parsley Flan, Date & Walnut Flan, Sweet Pear & Ginger Pastries, and Dairy-free Mushroom Pie.

Cakes & Cookies

Transform traditional cakes and cookies into a real tea-time extravaganza with some new adaptations of old tea-time favorites in Chapters 1 and 2. Irresistible cake recipes, such as Chocolate & Orange Ring, Mixed Fruit Cake, Spiced Apple Gingerbread, and Spiced Apple Cream Shortcakes, are included along with delicious cookie recipes, such as Dark Chocolate Chip & Vanilla Cookies, and Orange Gingernuts. These are quick and easy to make and are sure to be winners with all the family.

Making Cakes

With all baking recipes, some basic principles apply and this is especially true of cake making:

• First of all make sure that you read the recipe all the way through.

• Weigh all ingredients accurately and do basic preparation, such as grating and chopping, before starting to cook.

• Basic cake-making ingredients should be kept at room temperature.

• Mixtures that are creamed together, such as butter and sugar, should be almost white and have a "soft dropping" consistency. Creaming can be done by hand, but a hand-held electric mixer saves time and effort.

• "Folding in" is achieved by using a metal spoon or spatula and working as gently as possible to fold through the flour or dry ingredients in a figure of eight movement.

• Do not remove a cake from the oven until it is fully cooked. To test if a cake is cooked, press the surface lightly with your fingertips—it should feel springy to the touch. Alternatively, insert a fine metal skewer into the center of the cake—it will come out clean if the cake is cooked through.

• Let cakes cool a little in their pans before carefully turning out onto a wire rack to cool completely.

Making Pies & Tarts

When making the pies or tarts in this book, follow these basic principles:

1. Sift the dry ingredients into a large mixing bowl, add the diced fat, and toss it through the flour.

2. Gently rub the fat between your fingertips, a little at a time, until the mixture looks like fine bread crumbs. As you rub in the mixture, lift up your hands to aerate the mixture as it falls back into the bowl.

3. Bind the mixture with iced water or other specified liquid, using just enough to make a soft dough. Wrap the dough and let chill for at least 30 minutes.

Baking with Chocolate

Chocolate is produced from the beans of the cacao tree, which originated in South America, but now grows in Africa, the West Indies, the tropical parts of America, and the Far East. Cacao beans are large pods — once harvested, both the pulp from the pods and the bean are allowed to ferment in the sun. The pulp evaporates and the bean develops its chocolate flavor. The outer skin is then removed and the beans are left in the sun for a little longer, or roasted. Finally, they are shelled and the nibs are used for making cocoa and chocolate.

The nibs have to be ground and processed to produce a thick mixture or paste called "cocoa solids" and it is this mixture that we use to gauge the quality of chocolate. The cocoa solids are then pressed to remove some of the fat called "cocoa butter". They are then processed again to produce the product that we know and love as chocolate.

Storing Chocolate

Store chocolate in a cool, dry place away from direct heat or sunlight. Most chocolate can be stored for about 1 year. It can be kept in the refrigerator, but make sure it is well wrapped because it will pick up flavors from other foods. Chocolate decorations can be stored in airtight containers and interleaved with nonstick baking parchment. Dark chocolate will keep for 4 weeks and milk and white chocolate for 2 weeks.

Melting Chocolate

Chocolate should not be melted over direct heat, except when melted with other ingredients and even then the heat should be very low. Break the chocolate into small, equal-size pieces and put them in a heatproof bowl. Place the bowl over a pan of hot water on low heat, making sure the bottom is not in contact with the water. Once the chocolate starts to melt, stir gently and, if necessary, let it stand over the water a little longer. No drops of water or steam should come into contact with the melted chocolate because it will solidify.

To melt chocolate in a microwave oven, break the chocolate into small pieces and place in a microwave-proof bowl. Timing will vary according to the type and quantity of chocolate. As a guide, melt 4½ oz dark chocolate on High for 2 minutes, and white or milk chocolate on Medium for 2–3 minutes. Stir the chocolate and let stand for a few minutes, then stir again. Return to the microwave oven for another 30 seconds if necessary.

Setting Chocolate

Chocolate sets best at 65°F, although it will set (more slowly) in a slightly hotter room. If possible, set chocolate for decorations in a cool room. If set in the refrigerator it may develop a white bloom.

Types of Chocolate

Dark chocolate can contain anything from 30% to 75% cocoa solids. It has a slightly sweet flavor and a dark color. It is the chocolate most used in cooking. For everyday cooking and the majority of those recipes calling for dark chocolate, choose one with around 50% cocoa solids. However, dark chocolate with a higher cocoa solid content will give a richer, more intense flavor. This chocolate is often called luxury or continental chocolate and has a cocoa solid content of between 70–75%. Occasionally it is necessary to use a better chocolate and the individual recipes indicate where this is the case.

Milk chocolate, as its name suggests, contains milk and has a lovely creamy, mild, and sweet flavor. It is mostly used as an eating chocolate, rather than in cooking. However, it does have its place in chocolate cooking, especially for decorations and when a milder, creamier flavor is required. It is more sensitive to heat than dark chocolate so care must be taken when melting.

White chocolate contains a lower cocoa butter and cocoa solid content. It can be quite temperamental when used in cooking. Always choose a luxury white cooking chocolate to avoid problems and take great care not to overheat when melting. White chocolate is useful for color contrast, especially when decorating cakes.

Couverture chocolate is the preferred chocolate for professionals (it retains a high gloss after melting and cooling) but it requires tempering (stabilising) and is only available from speciality suppliers; it has therefore not been used in this book.

Chocolate-flavored cake covering is an inferior product not generally used by true chocolate lovers. However, it has a higher fat content making it easier to handle when making some decorations, such as curls or caraque. If you do not want to compromise the flavor too much, but have difficulty making the decorations with pure chocolate, try adding a few squares of chocolate-flavored cake covering to a good quality chocolate.

Chocolate chips are available in dark, milk, and white chocolate varieties and are used for baking and decoration.

Cocoa powder is the powder left after the cocoa butter has been pressed from the roasted and ground beans. It is unsweetened and bitter in flavor (not to be confused with the powdered cocoa beverage, which is sweetened). It gives a good, strong chocolate flavor when used in cooking.

Family Favorites

Experience the sweet pleasure of a wonderful selection of everyday and special occasion desserts and rich, gooey and irresistible puddings in Chapter 3, such as Mixed Fruit Pavlova, Chocolate Butter Cream Trifle, Orange & Marmalade Meringue, and Caramelised Cream Tartlets. Your favorite is sure to be included. This chapter also helps you to perfect your pastry so that you are guaranteed success with such timeless appetizing cookery classics as Lemon Tart, Cranberry & Almond Tart, and Mixed Fruit Crumble.

It is hard to resist the pleasure
of a sumptuous piece of cake and
no book on baking would be complete
without a selection of family cakes—
there are plenty to choose from in
this chapter. You can spend several
indulgent hours in the kitchen making that perfect

extravagant layer cake or pop into the
kitchen to knock up a quick cake for
an afternoon snack; the choice is yours.
The more experimental among you can vary
the fillings or decorations according to
what takes your fancy. Try dusting with

unsweetened cocoa instead of confectioners'
sugar, or sprinkling over some chopped mixed
nuts or candied fruit.

cakes

sweet pear sponge cake

What could be better than the lovely combination used in this cake of chocolate and fresh pears in a moist sponge?

Serves 6

¾ cup butter, softened

1 cup soft brown sugar

3 eggs, beaten

1¼ cups self-rising flour

2 tbsp unsweetened cocoa

2 tbsp milk

2 small pears, peeled, cored, and sliced

cook's tip

Serve the cake with melted chocolate drizzled over the top for a delicious dessert.

2

4

6

1 Grease an 8-inch loose-bottomed cake pan and carefully line the bottom with baking parchment.

2 In a bowl, cream together the butter and soft brown sugar until pale and fluffy.

3 Gradually add the beaten eggs to the creamed mixture, beating well after each addition.

4 Sift the self-rising flour and unsweetened cocoa powder into the creamed mixture and fold in gently until all of the ingredients are combined.

5 Stir in the milk, then spoon the mixture into the prepared pan. Level the surface with the back of a spoon or a knife.

6 Arrange the pear slices on top of the cake mixture, arranging them in a radiating pattern.

7 Bake in a preheated oven, 350°F/180°C, for about 1 hour, or until the cake is just firm to the touch.

8 Let the cake cool in the pan, then transfer to a wire rack until completely cold before serving.

jeweled sponge cake

This cake is extremely colorful; you can choose any mixture of candied fruits or stick to just one type if you prefer.

Serves 8

¾ cup butter, softened

¾ cup superfine sugar

3 eggs, beaten

6 oz self-rising flour, sifted

2 tbsp ground rice

finely grated rind of 1 lemon

4 tbsp lemon juice

⅔ cup candied fruits, chopped

confectioners' sugar, for dusting (optional)

1 Lightly grease a 7-inch cake pan and line carefully with baking parchment.

2 In a bowl, whisk together the butter and superfine sugar until fluffy.

3 Add the beaten eggs a little at a time. Using a metal spoon, fold in the flour and ground rice.

4 Add the grated lemon rind and juice, followed by the chopped candied fruits. Lightly mix all the ingredients together.

5 Spoon the mixture into the prepared pan and level the surface with the back of a spoon or a knife.

2

3

6 Bake in a preheated oven, 350°F, for 1 hour–1 hour 10 minutes until well risen or until a fine skewer inserted into the center of the cake comes out clean.

7 Let the cake cool in the pan for 5 minutes, before turning it out on to a wire rack to cool completely.

8 Dust well with confectioners' sugar, if using, before serving.

4

cook's tip

Wash and dry the candied fruits before chopping them. This will prevent the fruits sinking to the bottom of the cake during cooking.

marbled chocolate & orange ring

Separate chocolate and orange cake mixtures are combined in a ring mold to achieve the marbled effect in this light sponge.

5

6

7

Serves 8

¾ cup butter, softened

¾ cup superfine sugar

3 eggs, beaten

1¼ cups self-rising flour, sifted

¼ cup unsweetened cocoa, sifted

5–6 tbsp orange juice

grated rind of 1 orange

1 Lightly grease a 10-inch ovenproof ring mold.

2 In a mixing bowl, cream together the butter and sugar with an electric whisk for about 5 minutes.

3 Add the beaten egg a little at a time, whisking well after each addition.

4 Using a metal spoon, fold the flour into the creamed mixture carefully, then spoon half of the mixture into a separate mixing bowl.

5 Fold the unsweetened cocoa and half of the orange juice into one bowl and mix gently.

6 Fold the orange rind and remaining orange juice into the other bowl and mix gently.

7 Place spoonfuls of each of the mixtures alternately into the mold, then drag a skewer through the mixture to create a marbled effect.

8 Bake in a preheated oven, 350°F, for 30–35 minutes, or until well risen and a skewer inserted into the center comes out clean.

9 Let the cake cool in the mold before turning out carefully on to a wire rack.

variation

For a richer chocolate flavor, add 1³/₄oz chocolate drops to the cocoa mixture.

clementine & almond butter cake

This cake is flavored with clementine rind and juice, creating a rich buttery cake but one full of fresh fruit flavor.

Serves 8

2 clementines

¾ cup butter, softened

¾ cup superfine sugar

3 eggs, beaten

1½ cups self-rising flour

3 tbsp ground almonds

3 tbsp light cream

GLAZE AND TOPPING

6 tbsp clementine juice

2 tbsp superfine sugar

3 white sugar cubes, crushed

cook's tip

If you prefer, chop the rind from the clementines in a food processor or blender together with the sugar in step 2. Tip the mixture into a bowl with the butter and begin to cream the mixture.

2

4

1 Grease a 7-inch round pan and line the bottom with baking parchment.

2 Pare the rind from the clementines and chop the rind finely. In a bowl, cream together the butter, sugar, and clementine rind until pale and fluffy.

3 Gradually add the beaten eggs to the mixture, beating well after each addition.

4 Gently fold in the self-rising flour followed by the ground almonds and the light cream. Spoon the mixture into the prepared pan.

5 Bake in a preheated oven, 350°F, for about 55–60 minutes, or until a fine skewer inserted into the center comes out clean. Let cool slightly.

6 Meanwhile, make the glaze. Put the clementine juice into a small pan

7

with the superfine sugar. Bring to a boil and simmer for 5 minutes.

7 Drizzle the glaze over the cake until it has been absorbed and sprinkle with the crushed sugar cubes.

crunchy coffee sponge cake

This cake has a moist coffee sponge on the bottom, covered with a crisp, crunchy, spicy topping.

Serves 8

1¼ cups all-purpose flour

1 tbsp baking powder

⅓ cup superfine sugar

⅔ cup milk

2 eggs

½ cup butter, melted and cooled

2 tbsp instant coffee mixed with
   1 tbsp boiling water

½ cup almonds, chopped

confectioners' sugar, for dusting

TOPPING

½ cup self-rising flour

½ cup brown crystal sugar

6 tsp butter, cut into
   small pieces

1 tsp ground allspice

1 tbsp water

1 Grease a 9-inch loose-bottomed round cake pan and line carefully with baking parchment. Sift together the flour and baking powder into a mixing bowl, then stir in the superfine sugar.

2 Whisk the milk, eggs, butter, and coffee mixture together and pour on to the dry ingredients. Add the chopped almonds and mix lightly together. Spoon the mixture into the cake pan.

2

2

4

3 To make the topping, mix the flour and brown crystal sugar together in a separate bowl.

4 Rub in the butter with your fingers until the mixture is crumbly. Sprinkle in the ground allspice and the water and bring the mixture together in loose crumbs. Sprinkle the topping over the cake mixture.

5 Bake in a preheated oven, 375°F, for 50–60 minutes. Cover loosely with foil if the topping starts to brown too quickly. Let cool in the pan, then turn out. Dust with confectioners' sugar just before serving.

lemon sponge cake

The lovely light and tangy flavor of the sponge is balanced by the lemony syrup poured over the top of the cake.

3

Serves 8

1¾ cups all-purpose flour

2 tsp baking powder

1 cup superfine sugar

4 eggs

⅔ cup sour cream

grated rind 1 large lemon

4 tbsp lemon juice

⅔ cup sunflower oil

SYRUP

4 tbsp confectioners' sugar

3 tbsp lemon juice

4

7

cook's tip

Pricking the surface of the hot cake with a skewer ensures that the syrup seeps right into the cake and the full flavor is absorbed.

1 Lightly grease an 8-inch loose-bottomed round cake pan and line the base with baking parchment.

2 Sift the flour and baking powder into a mixing bowl and stir in the superfine sugar.

3 In a separate bowl, whisk the eggs, sour cream, lemon rind, lemon juice, and oil together.

4 Pour the egg mixture into the dry ingredients and mix well until evenly combined.

5 Pour the mixture into the prepared pan and bake in a preheated oven, 350°F, for 45–60 minutes, or until risen and golden brown.

6 Meanwhile, to make the syrup, mix together the confectioners' sugar and lemon juice in a small pan. Stir over a low heat until just beginning to bubble and turn syrupy.

7 As soon as the cake comes out of the oven, prick the surface with a fine skewer, then brush the syrup over the top. Let the cake cool completely in the pan before turning out and serving.

spiced apple gingerbread

This spicy gingerbread is made even more moist by the addition of chopped fresh apples.

Makes 12 bars

⅔ cup butter

1 cup soft brown sugar

2 tbsp molasses

2 cups all-purpose flour

1 tsp baking powder

2 tsp baking soda

2 tsp ground ginger

⅔ cup milk

1 egg, beaten

2 dessert apples, peeled, chopped, and
    coated with 1 tbsp lemon juice

1 Grease a 9-inch square cake pan
   and line with baking parchment.

2 Melt the butter, sugar, and
   molasses in a pan over low heat
and let the mixture cool.

3 Sift the flour, baking powder,
   baking soda, and ginger into a
mixing bowl.

2

5

4 Stir in the milk, beaten egg, and
   cooled buttery liquid, followed by
the chopped apples coated with the
lemon juice.

5 Mix everything together gently,
   then pour the mixture into the
prepared pan.

6 Bake in a preheated oven, 325°F,
   for 30–35 minutes, or until the cake
has risen and a fine skewer inserted
into the center comes out clean.

7 Let the cake cool in the pan
   before turning out and cutting into
12 bars.

variation

If you enjoy the flavor of
ginger, try adding 1 oz
candied ginger, chopped
finely, to the mixture in
step 3.

traditional pound cake

This is a classic pound cake made in the traditional way with caraway seeds. If you do not like their flavor, they can be omitted.

2

Serves 4

1 cup butter, softened

1 cup soft brown sugar

3 eggs, beaten

3 cups self-rising flour

1 tbsp caraway seeds

grated rind of 1 lemon

6 tbsp milk

1 or 2 strips of citron peel

4

5

cook's tip

Citron peel is available in the baking section of supermarkets. If it is unavailable, you can substitute it with chopped mixed peel.

1 Grease and line a 2-lb loaf pan.

2 In a bowl, cream together the butter and soft brown sugar until pale and fluffy.

3 Gradually add the beaten eggs to the creamed mixture, beating well after each addition.

4 Sift the flour into the bowl. Gently fold into the creamed mixture.

5 Add the caraway seeds, lemon rind, and the milk and fold in until thoroughly blended.

6 Spoon the mixture into the pan and level the surface.

7 Bake in a preheated oven, 325°F, for 20 minutes.

8 Remove the cake from the oven. Place the pieces of citron peel on top of the cake and return it to the oven for another 40 minutes, or until the cake is well risen and a fine skewer inserted into the center comes out clean.

9 Let the cake cool in the pan before turning out and transferring to a wire rack until completely cold.

glazed honey & almond cake

Being glazed with a honey syrup after baking gives this almond-flavored cake a lovely moist texture, but it can be eaten without the glaze, if preferred.

Serves 8

⅓ cup soft tub margarine

3 tbsp soft brown sugar

2 eggs

1½ cups self-rising flour

1 tsp baking powder

4 tbsp milk

2 tbsp liquid honey

½ cup slivered almonds

SYRUP

⅔ cup runny honey

2 tbsp lemon juice

cook's tip

Experiment with different flavored honeys for the syrup glaze until you find one that you think tastes best.

2

3

6

1 Grease a 7-inch round cake pan and line with baking parchment.

2 Place the margarine, brown sugar, eggs, flour, baking powder, milk, and honey in a large mixing bowl and beat well with a wooden spoon for 1 minute, or until all of the ingredients are thoroughly mixed together.

3 Spoon into the prepared pan and level the surface with the back of a spoon or a spatula, then sprinkle with the almonds.

4 Bake in a preheated oven, 350°F, for about 50 minutes, or until the cake is well risen.

5 Meanwhile, make the syrup. Combine the honey and lemon juice in a small pan and simmer for about 5 minutes, or until the syrup starts to coat the back of a spoon.

6 As soon as the cake comes out of the oven, pour over the syrup, letting it seep into the middle of the warm cake.

7 Let the cake cool for at least 2 hours before slicing.

rich chocolate cake

This chocolate cake gets its moist texture from the
sour cream that is stirred into the beaten mixture.

1

Serves 10-12

1 cup butter

3½ oz dark chocolate, chopped

⅔ cup water

2½ cups all-purpose flour

2 tsp baking powder

1¾ cups soft brown sugar

⅔ cup sour cream

2 eggs, beaten

FROSTING

7 oz dark chocolate

6 tbsp water

3 tbsp light cream

1 tbsp butter, chilled

1 Grease a 13 x 5 x 3¼-inch square cake pan and line the bottom with baking parchment. In a separate pan, melt the butter and chocolate with the water over low heat, stirring the mixture frequently.

3

2 Sift the flour and baking powder into a mixing bowl and stir in the brown sugar.

3 Pour the hot chocolate liquid into the bowl and beat well until all of the ingredients are evenly mixed. Stir in the sour cream, followed by the eggs.

4 Pour the mixture into the prepared pan and bake in a preheated oven, 375°F, for 40–45 minutes.

5 Let the cake cool in the pan before turning it out on to a wire rack. Let it cool completely.

6 To make the frosting, melt the chocolate with the water in a pan over very low heat, then stir in the cream and remove from the heat. Stir in the chilled butter, then pour the frosting over the cooled cake, using a spatula to spread it evenly over the top of the cake.

cook's tip

Stand the cake on the wire rack to frost it and place a large cookie sheet underneath to catch any drips.

3

chocolate cake with almonds

Chocolate and almonds complement each other perfectly in this delicious cake. Be warned, one slice will never be enough!

Serves 8-10

6 oz dark chocolate

¾ cup butter

4½ oz superfine sugar

4 eggs, separated

¼ tsp cream of tartar

½ cup self-rising flour

1¼ cups ground almonds

1 tsp almond extract

TOPPING

4½ oz milk chocolate

2 tbsp butter

4 tbsp heavy cream

TO DECORATE

2 tbsp toasted slivered almonds

1 oz dark chocolate, melted

1 Lightly grease and line the base of a 9-inch round springform pan. Break the chocolate into small pieces and place in a small pan with the butter. Heat gently, stirring until melted and well combined.

2

2 Place 7 tbsp of the superfine sugar in a bowl with the egg yolks and whisk until pale and creamy. Add the melted chocolate mixture, beating until well combined.

3 Sift the cream of tartar and flour together and fold into the chocolate mixture with the ground almonds and almond extract.

4 Whisk the egg whites in a bowl until standing in soft peaks. Add the remaining superfine sugar and whisk for about 2 minutes by hand, or 45–60 seconds, if using an electric whisk, until thick and glossy. Fold the egg whites into the chocolate mixture and spoon into the pan. Bake in a preheated oven, 375°F, for 40 minutes, or until just springy to the touch. Let cool.

4

4

5 Heat the topping ingredients in a bowl over a pan of hot water. Remove from the heat and beat for 2 minutes. Let chill for 30 minutes. Transfer the cake to a plate and spread with the topping. Scatter with the almonds and drizzle with melted chocolate. Let stand for 2 hours before serving.

creamy coffee cake

Chocolate cake and a creamy coffee-flavored filling
are combined in this delicious mocha cake.

Serves 8-10

1 cup self-rising flour

¼ tsp baking powder

4 tbsp unsweetened cocoa

7 tbsp superfine sugar

2 eggs

2 tbsp light corn syrup

⅔ cup sunflower oil

⅔ cup milk

FILLING

1 tsp instant coffee

1 tbsp boiling water

1¼ cups heavy cream

2 tbsp confectioners' sugar

TO DECORATE

1¾ oz grated chocolate

chocolate caraque (see page 249)

confectioners' sugar, to dust

2

4

5

1 Lightly grease three 7-inch cake pans.

2 Sift the flour, baking powder, and unsweetened cocoa into a large mixing bowl. Stir in the sugar. Make a well in the center and stir in the eggs, syrup, sunflower oil, and milk. Beat with a wooden spoon, gradually mixing in the dry ingredients to make a smooth batter. Divide the mixture between the prepared pans.

3 Bake in a preheated oven, 350°F, for 35–45 minutes, or until springy to the touch. Let stand in the pans for 5 minutes, then turn out on to a wire rack to cool completely.

4 Dissolve the instant coffee in the boiling water and place in a bowl with the cream and confectioners' sugar. Whip until the cream is just holding it's shape. Use half of the cream to sandwich the 3 cakes together. Spread the remaining cream over the top and sides of the cake. Lightly press the grated chocolate into the cream around the edge of the cake.

5 Transfer to a serving plate. Lay the caraque over the top of the cake. Cut a few thin strips of baking parchment and place on top of the caraque. Dust lightly with confectioners' sugar, then carefully remove the parchment. Serve.

mixed fruit cake

It is well worth using a good-quality olive oil for this cake, because this will determine its flavor. The cake will keep well in an airtight tin until ready to eat.

Serves 8

2 cups self-rising flour

9 tsp superfine sugar

½ cup milk

4 tbsp orange juice

⅔ cup olive oil

3½ oz mixed dried fruit

1 oz pine nuts

1 Grease a 7-inch cake pan and line it with baking parchment.

2 Sift the flour into a mixing bowl and stir in the superfine sugar.

3 Make a well in the center of the dry ingredients and pour in the milk and orange juice. Stir the mixture with a wooden spoon, gradually beating in the flour and sugar.

4 Pour in the olive oil, stirring until the ingredients are evenly mixed.

3

4

5

5 Stir the mixed dried fruit and pine nuts into the mixture and spoon into the prepared pan.

6 Bake in a preheated oven, 350°F, for about 45 minutes, or until the cake is golden and firm to the touch.

7 Let the cake cool in the pan for a few minutes before transferring to a wire rack to cool.

8 Serve the cake warm or cold and cut into slices.

cook's tip

Pine nuts are best known as one of the ingredients in the classic Italian pesto, but here they give a delicate, slightly resinous flavor to this cake.

classic carrot cake

This classic favorite is always popular with children
and adults alike when it is served as an afternoon snack.

2

Makes 12 bars

1 cup self-rising flour

pinch of salt

1 tsp ground cinnamon

¼ cup soft brown sugar

2 eggs

scant ½ cup sunflower oil

4½ oz carrot, peeled and finely grated

½ cup shredded coconut

½ cup walnuts, chopped

walnut pieces, for decoration

FROSTING

10 tsp butter, softened

1¾ oz full-fat soft cheese

1½ cups confectioners' sugar, sifted

1 tsp lemon juice

3

1 Lightly grease an 8-inch square cake pan and line carefully with baking parchment.

2 Sift the flour, salt, and ground cinnamon into a large bowl and stir in the brown sugar. Add the eggs and oil to the dry ingredients and mix well.

3 Stir in the grated carrot, shredded coconut, and chopped walnuts.

4 Pour the mixture into the prepared pan and bake in a preheated oven, 350°F, for 20–25 minutes, or until just firm to the touch. Let cool in the pan.

5 Meanwhile, make the cheese frosting. In a bowl, beat together the butter, full-fat soft cheese, confectioners' sugar, and lemon juice, until the mixture is fluffy and creamy.

5

6 Turn the cake out of the pan and cut into 12 bars or slices. Spread with the frosting and then decorate with walnut pieces.

variation

For a more moist cake, replace the coconut with 1 roughly mashed banana.

golden fruit cake

The cornmeal adds texture to this fruit cake, as well as an interesting golden yellow color. It also acts as a flour, binding the ingredients together to create a lighter consistency.

Serves 8-10

⅓ cup butter, softened

½ cup superfine sugar

2 eggs, beaten

⅓ cup self-rising flour, sifted

⅔ cup cornmeal

1 tsp baking powder

8 oz mixed dried fruit

1oz pine nuts

grated rind of 1 lemon

4 tbsp lemon juice

2 tbsp milk

variation

To give a more crumbly light fruit cake, omit the cornmeal and use 1¼ cups self-rising flour instead.

2

3

5

4 Fold the flour, baking powder, and cornmeal into the mixture until well blended.

5 Stir in the mixed dried fruit, pine nuts, grated lemon rind, lemon juice, and milk.

6 Spoon the mixture into the prepared pan and level the surface.

1 Grease a 7-inch cake pan and line the base with baking parchment.

2 In a bowl, whisk together the butter and sugar until light and fluffy.

3 Whisk in the beaten eggs gradually, whisking well after each addition.

7 Bake in a preheated oven, 350°F, for about 1 hour, or until a fine skewer inserted into the center of the cake comes out clean.

8 Let the cake cool in the pan before turning out.

rum & chocolate sponge cake

Soft chocolatey sponge topped with a rich chocolate truffle mixture makes a cake that chocoholics will die for.

Serves 12

⅓ cup butter

⅓ cup superfine sugar

2 eggs, lightly beaten

⅔ cup self-rising flour

½ tsp baking powder

¼ cup unsweetened cocoa

1¾ oz ground almonds

TRUFFLE TOPPING

12 oz dark chocolate

3½ oz butter

1¼ cups heavy cream

1¼ cups plain cake crumbs

3 tbsp dark rum

TO DECORATE

ground cherries

1¾ oz dark chocolate, melted

1 Lightly grease an 8-inch round springform pan and line the bottom. Beat together the butter and sugar until light and fluffy. Gradually add the eggs, beating well after each addition.

2 Sift together the flour, baking powder, and unsweetened cocoa and fold into the mixture along with the ground almonds. Pour into the prepared pan and bake in a preheated oven, 350°F, for 20–25 minutes, or until springy to the touch. Let cool slightly in the pan, then transfer to a wire rack to cool completely. Wash and dry the pan and return the cooled cake to the pan.

3 To make the topping, heat the chocolate, butter, and cream in a heavy-bottomed pan over a low heat and stir until smooth. Cool, then chill for 30 minutes. Beat well with a wooden spoon and chill for another 30 minutes. Beat the mixture again, then add the cake crumbs and rum, beating until well combined. Spoon over the sponge base and chill for 3 hours.

4 Meanwhile, dip the ground cherries in the melted chocolate until partially covered. Let stand on baking parchment to set. Transfer the cake to a serving plate; decorate with ground cherries.

chocolate & almond layer cake

Thin layers of delicious light chocolate cake sandwiched together with a rich chocolate frosting.

3

Serves 10-12

7 eggs

1¾ cups superfine sugar

1¼ cups all-purpose flour

½ cup unsweetened cocoa

4 tbsp butter, melted

FILLING

7 oz dark chocolate

½ cup butter

4 tbsp confectioners' sugar

TO DECORATE

10 tbsp toasted slivered almonds, crushed
  lightly

small chocolate curls (see page 240) or
  grated chocolate

5

5

1 Grease a deep 9-inch square cake
  pan and line the base with baking
parchment.

2 Whisk the eggs and superfine sugar
  in a mixing bowl with an electric
whisk for about 10 minutes, or until the
mixture is very light and foamy and the
whisk leaves a trail that lasts a few
seconds when lifted.

3 Sift the flour and cocoa together and
  fold half into the mixture. Drizzle over
the melted butter and fold in the rest of
the flour and cocoa. Pour into the
prepared pan and bake in a preheated
oven, 350°F, for 30–35 minutes, or until
springy to the touch. Let cool slightly,
then remove from the pan and cool
completely on a wire rack.

4 To make the filling, melt the
  chocolate and butter together, then
remove from the heat. Stir in the
confectioners' sugar and let cool, then
beat until thick enough to spread.

5 Halve the cake lengthwise and cut
  each half into 3 layers. Sandwich the
layers together with three-fourths of the
chocolate filling. Spread the remainder
over the cake and mark a wavy pattern
on the top. Press the almonds
on to the sides. Decorate with chocolate
curls or grated chocolate.

layered mango cake

Peaches can be used instead of mangoes for this deliciously moist cake, if you prefer. If the top of the cake is very domed, cut a piece off, then turn the cake upside down so that you have a flat surface to decorate.

2

3

Serves 12

⅓ cup unsweetened cocoa

⅔ cup boiling water

6 large eggs

1½ cups superfine sugar

2½ cups self-rising flour

28 oz canned mango

1 tsp cornstarch

generous 1½ cups heavy cream

2½ oz grated chocolate

6

1 Grease a deep 9-inch round cake pan and line the base with baking parchment.

2 Place the unsweetened cocoa in a small bowl and gradually add the boiling water; blend together to form a smooth paste.

3 Place the eggs and superfine sugar in a mixing bowl and whisk until the mixture is very light and foamy and the whisk leaves a trail that lasts a few seconds when lifted. Fold in the cocoa mixture. Sift the flour and fold it into the mixture.

4 Pour the mixture into the pan and level the top. Bake in a preheated oven, 325°F, for about 1 hour, or until springy to the touch.

5 Let cool in the pan for a few minutes, then turn out and cool completely on a wire rack. Peel off the lining paper and cut the cake carefully into 3 layers.

6 Drain the mangoes and place one fourth of them in a food processor and purée until smooth. Mix the cornstarch with about 3 tbsp of the mango juice to form a smooth paste. Add to the mango purée. Transfer to a small pan and heat gently, stirring until the purée thickens. Let cool.

7 Chop the remaining mango. Whip the cream and reserve about one fourth. Fold the mango into the remaining cream and use to sandwich the layers of cake together. Place on a serving plate. Spread some of the remaining cream around the side of the cake. Press the grated chocolate lightly into the cream. Pipe cream rosettes around the top. Spread the mango purée over the center.

lamington cake with coconut

This cake is based on the famous Australian Lamington cake (named after Lord Lamington, a former Governor of Queensland), which has chocolate frosting covered with coconut.

Serves 8-10

¾ cup butter or block margarine

¾ cup superfine sugar

3 eggs, lightly beaten

1¼ cups self-rising flour

2 tbsp unsweetened cocoa

1¾ oz dark chocolate, broken, into pieces

5 tbsp milk

1 tsp butter

¾ cup confectioners' sugar

about 8 tbsp shredded coconut

¼ pint heavy cream, whipped

4

5

5

1 Lightly grease a 1-lb loaf pan—preferably a long, thin pan about 10 inches long by 3 inches wide.

2 Cream together the butter and sugar in a bowl until light and fluffy. Gradually add the eggs, beating well after each addition. Sift together the flour and cocoa. Fold into the mixture.

3 Pour the mixture into the prepared pan and level the top. Bake in a preheated oven, 350°F, for 40 minutes, or until springy to the touch. Let cool for 5 minutes in the pan, then turn out on to a wire rack to cool completely.

4 Place the chocolate, milk, and butter in a heatproof bowl set over a pan of hot water. Stir until the chocolate has melted. Add the confectioners' sugar and beat until smooth. Let cool until the frosting is thick enough to spread, then spread it all over the cake. Sprinkle with the coconut and let the frosting set.

5 Cut a V-shape wedge from the top of the cake. Put the cream into a pastry bag fitted with a plain or star tip. Pipe the cream down the center of the wedge and replace the wedge of cake on top of the cream. Pipe another line of cream down either side of the wedge of cake. Serve.

frosted chocolate butter cake

This walnut-studded chocolate cake has a tasty chocolate butter frosting. It is perfect for serving at coffee mornings, because it can be made the day before.

Serves 8-12

4 eggs

½ cup superfine sugar

1 cup all-purpose flour

1 tbsp unsweetened cocoa

2 tbsp butter, melted

2¾ oz dark chocolate, melted

1¼ cups finely chopped walnuts

FROSTING

2¾ oz dark chocolate

½ cup butter

1¼ cups confectioners' sugar

2 tbsp milk

walnut halves, to decorate

2

5

3 Let cool in the pan for 5 minutes, then transfer to a wire rack to cool completely. Cut the cold cake into 2 layers.

1 Grease a 7-inch deep round cake pan and line the base. Place the eggs and superfine sugar in a mixing bowl and whisk with electric beaters for 10 minutes, or until the mixture is light and foamy and the whisk leaves a trail that lasts a few seconds when lifted.

4 To make the frosting, melt the dark chocolate and let cool slightly. Beat together the butter, confectioners' sugar, and milk in a bowl until the mixture is pale and fluffy. Whisk in the melted chocolate.

5

2 Sift together the flour and unsweetened cocoa and fold in with a metal spoon or spatula. Fold in the melted butter and chocolate, and the chopped walnuts. Pour into the prepared pan and bake in a preheated oven, 325°F, and bake for 30–35 minutes, or until springy to the touch.

5 Sandwich the 2 cake layers with some of the frosting and place on a serving plate. Spread the remaining frosting over the top of the cake with a spatula, swirling it slightly as you do so. Decorate the cake with the walnut halves and serve.

creamy white chocolate cake

A light white sponge, topped with a rich creamy-white chocolate truffle mixture, makes an out-of-this-world layer cake.

Serves 12

2 eggs

4 tbsp superfine sugar

⅛ cup all-purpose flour

1¾ oz white chocolate, melted

TRUFFLE TOPPIING

1¼ cups heavy cream

12 oz white chocolate, broken into pieces

9 oz Quark low-fat curd cheese or cream cheese

TO DECORATE

dark, milk, or white chocolate, melted

unsweetened cocoa, to dust

1 Grease an 8-inch round springform pan and line the bottom. Whisk the eggs and superfine sugar in a mixing bowl for 10 minutes, or until the mixture is very light and foamy and the whisk leaves a trail that lasts a few seconds when lifted. Sift the flour and fold in with a metal spoon. Fold in the melted white chocolate. Pour into the pan and bake in a preheated oven, 350°F, for 25 minutes, or until springy to the touch. Let cool slightly, then transfer to a wire rack until completely cold. Return the cold cake to the pan.

2 To make the topping, place the cream in a pan and bring to a boil, stirring to prevent it sticking to the bottom of the pan. Cool slightly, then

add the white chocolate pieces and stir until melted and combined. Remove from the heat and let stand until almost cool, stirring, then stir in the Quark or cream cheese. Pour the mixture on top of the cake and chill for 2 hours. Remove the cake from the pan and transfer to a serving plate.

3 To make large chocolate curls, pour melted chocolate on to a marble or acrylic board and spread it thinly with a spatula. Let it set at room temperature. Using a scraper, push through the chocolate at a 25° angle until a large curl forms. Remove each curl as you make it and let chill until set. Decorate the cake with chocolate curls and sprinkle with a little unsweetened cocoa.

chocolate, carrot & walnut cake

What could be better than carrot and walnut cake with added chocolate? Rich and moist, this cake is marvelous as an afternoon snack.

Serves 10-12

5 eggs

½ cup superfine sugar

1¼ cups all-purpose flour

½ cup unsweetened cocoa

6 oz carrots, peeled and finely grated

½ cup chopped walnuts

2 tbsp sunflower oil

12 oz medium-fat soft cheese

1 cup confectioners' sugar

6 oz milk or dark chocolate, melted

1 Lightly grease and line the base of an 8-inch deep round cake pan.

2 Place the eggs and sugar in a large mixing bowl set over a pan of gently simmering water and whisk until very thick. Lift the whisk up and let the mixture drizzle back—it will leave a trail for a few seconds when thick enough.

3 Remove the bowl from the heat. Sift the flour and unsweetened cocoa into the bowl and fold in carefully. Then fold in the carrots, walnuts, and oil until just combined.

2

5

3

4 Pour into the prepared pan and bake in a preheated oven, 375°F, for 45 minutes, or until well risen and springy to the touch. Let cool slightly, then turn out onto a wire rack to cool completely.

5 Beat together the soft cheese and confectioners' sugar until combined. Beat in the melted chocolate. Split the cake in half and sandwich together again with half of the chocolate mixture. Cover the top of the cake with the remainder of the chocolate mixture, swirling it with a knife. Let chill or serve at once.

cook's tip

The undecorated cake can be frozen for up to 2 months. Defrost at room temperature for 3 hours or overnight in the refrigerator.

white chocolate cream cake

If you cannot decide if you prefer bitter dark chocolate or rich creamy white chocolate, then this delicious cake is for you.

Serves 10

4 eggs

7 tbsp cup superfine sugar

¾ cup all-purpose flour

DARK CHOCOLATE CREAM

⅔ cup heavy cream

5½ oz dark chocolate, broken into small
   pieces

WHITE CHOCOLATE FROSTING

2¾ oz white chocolate

1 tbsp butter

1 tbsp milk

4 tbsp confectioners' sugar

chocolate caraque (see page 249)

2

3

5

1 Grease an 8-inch round springform pan and line the bottom. Whisk the eggs and superfine sugar in a large mixing bowl with electric beaters for about 10 minutes, or until the mixture is very light and foamy and the whisk leaves a trail that lasts a few seconds when lifted.

2 Sift the flour and fold in with a metal spoon or spatula. Pour into the prepared pan and bake in a preheated oven, 350°F, for 35–40 minutes, or until springy to the touch. Let cool slightly, then transfer to a wire rack to cool completely. Cut into 2 layers.

3 To make the chocolate cream, place the cream in a pan and bring to a boil, stirring. Add the chocolate and stir until melted and well combined. Remove from the heat and let cool. Beat with a wooden spoon until thick.

4 Sandwich the 2 cake layers back together with the chocolate cream and place on a wire rack.

5 To make the frosting, melt the chocolate and butter together and stir until blended. Whisk in the milk and confectioners' sugar. Whisk for a few minutes until the frosting is cool. Pour it over the cake and spread with a spatula to coat the top and sides. Decorate with chocolate caraque and let set.

citrus mousse cake

With a dark chocolate sponge sandwiched together with a light, creamy, orange mousse, this spectacular cake is irresistible.

2

Serves 12

¼ cup butter

⅔ cup superfine sugar

4 eggs, lightly beaten

1¼ cups self-rising flour

1 tbsp unsweetened cocoa

1¼ oz dark orange-flavored chocolate,
   melted

ORANGE MOUSSE

2 eggs, separated

4 tbsp superfine sugar

⅔ cup freshly squeezed orange juice

2 tsp gelatin

3 tbsp water

1¼ cups heavy cream

peeled orange slices, to decorate

3

2 Pour into the prepared pan and level
the top. Bake in a preheated oven,
350°F, for 40 minutes, or until springy to
the touch. Let cool for 5 minutes in the
pan, then turn out and let cool
completely on a wire rack. Cut the cold
cake into 2 layers.

3 To make the orange mousse, beat
the egg yolks and sugar until light,
then whisk in the orange juice. Sprinkle
the gelatin over the water in a small bowl
and let it go spongy, then place over a
pan of hot water and stir until dissolved.
Stir into the mousse.

5

5 Place half of the cake in the pan.
Pour in the mousse and press the
second cake layer on top. Chill until set.
Transfer to a dish, then pipe cream
rosettes on the top and arrange orange
slices in the center.

1 Grease an 8-inch springform cake
pan and and line the bottom. Beat
the butter and sugar in a bowl until light
and fluffy. Gradually add the eggs,
beating well after each addition. Sift
together the flour and cocoa and then
fold into the cake mixture. Fold in the
melted chocolate.

4 Whip the cream until holding its
shape. Reserve a little for decoration
and fold the rest into the mousse. Whisk
the egg whites until standing in soft
peaks, then fold in. Let stand in a cool
place until starting to set, stirring
occasionally.

dark chocolate torte

This torte is perfect for serving on a hot sunny day with heavy cream and a selection of fresh summer berries.

Serves 10

8 oz dark chocolate, broken into pieces

3 tbsp water

1 cup soft brown sugar

¼ cup butter, softened

¼ cup ground almonds

3 tbsp self-rising flour

5 eggs, separated

¼ cup blanched almonds, chopped finely

confectioners' sugar, for dusting

heavy cream, to serve (optional)

2

3

3

1 Grease a 9-inch loose-bottomed cake pan and line the bottom with baking parchment.

2 In a pan set over very low heat, melt the chocolate with the water, stirring until smooth. Add the sugar and stir until dissolved, taking the pan off the heat to prevent it overheating.

3 Add the butter in small amounts until it has melted into the chocolate. Remove from the heat and lightly stir in the ground almonds and flour. Add the egg yolks one at a time, beating well after each addition.

4 In a large mixing bowl, whisk the egg whites until they stand in soft peaks, then fold them into the chocolate mixture with a metal spoon. Stir in the chopped almonds. Pour the mixture into the pan and level the surface.

5 Bake in a preheated oven, 350°F, for 40–45 minutes, or until well risen and firm (the cake will crack on the surface during cooking).

6 Let the cake cool in the pan for 30–40 minutes, then turn it out onto a wire rack to cool completely. Dust with confectioners' sugar and serve in slices with heavy cream, if using.

cook's tip

For a nuttier flavor, toast the chopped almonds in a dry skillet over a medium heat for about 2 minutes, or until lightly golden.

frosted chocolate orange cake

An all-time favorite combination of flavors means this cake is ideal for a snack-time treat. Omit the frosting, if preferred, and sprinkle instead with confectioners' sugar.

2

3

Serves 8-10

3⁄4 cup superfine sugar

¾ cup butter or block margarine

3 eggs, beaten

1½ cups self-rising flour, sifted

2 tbsp unsweetened cocoa, sifted

2 tbsp milk

3 tbsp orange juice

grated rind of ½ orange

FROSTING

1 cup confectioners' sugar

2 tbsp orange juice

4

variation

Add 2 tablespoons of rum or brandy to the chocolate mixture instead of the milk. The cake also works well when flavored with grated lemon rind and juice instead of the orange.

1 Lightly grease an 8-inch deep round cake pan.

2 Beat together the sugar and butter or margarine in a bowl until light and fluffy. Gradually add the eggs, beating well after each addition. Carefully fold in the flour.

3 Divide the mixture in half. Add the unsweetened cocoa and milk to one half, stirring until well mixed. Flavor the other half with the orange juice and rind.

4 Place spoonfuls of each mixture into the prepared pan and swirl together with a skewer, to create a marbled effect. Bake in a preheated oven, 375°F, for 25 minutes, until springy to the touch.

5 Let the cake cool in the pan for a few minutes before transferring to a wire rack to cool completely.

6 To make the frosting, sift the confectioners' sugar into a mixing bowl and mix in enough of the orange juice to form a smooth frosting. Spread the frosting over the top of the cake and let set before serving.

chocolate cream cake

Ganache—a divine mixture of chocolate and cream—is used to fill and decorate this rich chocolate cake, making it a chocolate-lover's dream.

Serves 10-12

¼ cup butter

⅔ cup superfine sugar

4 eggs, lightly beaten

1¾ cups self-rising flour

1 tbsp unsweetened cocoa

1¾ oz dark chocolate, melted

GANACHE

2 cups heavy cream

13 oz dark chocolate, broken into pieces

TO FINISH

7 oz chocolate-flavored cake covering

1

4

5

1 Lightly grease an 8-inch springform cake pan and line the bottom. Beat the butter and sugar until light and fluffy. Gradually add the eggs, beating well after each addition. Sift together the flour and cocoa. Fold into the cake mixture. Fold in the melted chocolate.

2 Pour into the prepared pan and level the top. Bake in a preheated oven, 350°F, for 40 minutes, or until springy to the touch. Let cool for 5 minutes in the pan, then turn out on to a wire rack and let cool completely. Cut the cold cake into 2 layers.

3 To make the ganache, place the cream in a pan and bring to a boil, stirring. Add the chocolate and stir until melted and combined. Pour into a bowl and whisk for about 5 minutes, or until the ganache is fluffy and cool.

4 Reserve one-third of the ganache. Use the remaining ganache to sandwich the cake together and spread over the top and sides of the cake.

5 Melt the cake covering and spread it over a large sheet of baking parchment. Cool until just set. Cut into strips a little wider than the height of the cake. Place the strips around the edge of the cake, overlapping them slightly.

6 Pipe the reserved ganache in tear drops or shells to cover the top of the cake. Chill for 1 hour.

viennese sachertorte

This rich, melt-in-the mouth cake originates in Austria. Make sure you have a steady hand when writing the name on the top. If preferred, you could drizzle a random scribble of chocolate instead.

Serves 10-12

6 oz dark chocolate

⅔ cup unsalted butter

⅔ cup superfine sugar

6 eggs, separated

1¼ cups all-purpose flour

FROSTING AND FILLING

6 oz dark chocolate

5 tbsp strong black coffee

1 cup confectioners' sugar

6 tbsp good apricot preserve

1¾ oz dark chocolate, melted

1

3

1 Grease a 9-inch springform cake pan and line the base. Melt the chocolate. Beat the butter and ⅓ cup of the sugar until pale and fluffy. Add the egg yolks and beat well. Add the chocolate in a thin stream, beating well. Sift the flour; fold it into the mixture. Whisk the egg whites until they stand in soft peaks. Add the remaining sugar and whisk for 2 minutes by hand, or 45–60 seconds if using an electric whisk, until glossy. Fold half into the chocolate mixture, then fold in the remainder.

4

2 Spoon into the prepared pan and level the top. Bake in a preheated oven, 300°F, for 1–1¼ hours, or until a skewer inserted into the center comes out clean. Cool in the pan for 5 minutes, then transfer to a wire rack to cool completely.

3 To make the frosting, melt the chocolate and beat in the coffee until smooth. Sift the confectioners' sugar into a bowl. Whisk in the melted chocolate mixture to give a thick frosting. Halve the cake. Warm the jam, then spread over one half of the cake and sandwich together. Invert the cake on a wire rack. Spoon the frosting over the cake and spread to coat the top and sides. Let it set for 5 minutes, letting any excess frosting drop through the rack. Transfer to a serving plate and let it set for at least 2 hours.

4 To decorate, spoon the melted chocolate into a small pastry bag and pipe the word "Sacher" or "Sachertorte" on the top of the cake. Let it harden before serving the cake.

crunchy glazed dobos torte

This wonderful cake originates from Hungary and consists of thin layers of light sponge sandwiched together with butter cream and topped with a crunchy caramel layer.

1

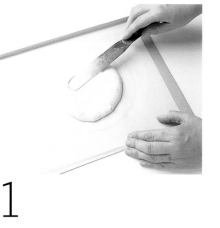

1

2

Serves 8

3 eggs

7 tbsp superfine sugar

1 tsp vanilla extract

½ cup all-purpose flour

FILLING

6 oz dark chocolate

¾ cup butter

2 tbsp milk

2 cups confectioners' sugar

CARAMEL

7 tbsp granulated sugar

4 tbsp water

1 Draw four 7-inch circles on sheets of baking parchment. Place 2 of them upside down on 2 cookie sheets. Whisk the eggs and superfine sugar in a large mixing bowl with electric beaters for 10 minutes, or until the mixture is light and foamy and the whisk leaves a trail. Fold in the vanilla extract. Sift the flour and fold in with a metal spoon or a spatula. Spoon one fourth of the mixture on to one of the sheets and spread out to the size of the circle. Repeat with the other circle. Bake in a preheated oven, 400°F, for 5–8 minutes, or until golden brown. Cool on wire racks. Repeat with the remaining mixture.

2 To make the filling, melt the chocolate and cool slightly. Beat the butter, milk, and confectioners' sugar until pale and fluffy. Whisk in the chocolate. Place the sugar and water for the caramel in a heavy-bottomed pan and heat gently, stirring until the sugar dissolves. Boil gently until the syrup is pale golden. Remove from the heat. Pour over one layer of the cake to cover the top. Let it harden slightly, then mark into 8 portions with an oiled knife. Remove the cakes from the parchment and trim the edges. Sandwich the layers together with some of the filling, finishing with the caramel-topped cake. Place on a serving plate and spread the sides with the filling mixture, using a comb scraper if you have one. Pipe rosettes around the top of the cake.

Russian torte

This is a Russian marbled chocolate cake which is soaked in a delicious flavored syrup and decorated with chocolate and cream.

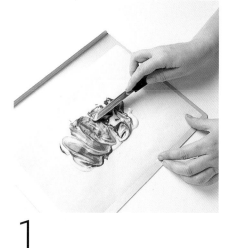

1

Serves 10

CHOCOLATE TRIANGLES

1 oz dark chocolate, melted

1 oz white chocolate, melted

CAKE

¾ cup soft margarine

¾ cup superfine sugar

½ tsp vanilla extract

3 eggs, lightly beaten

2 cups self-rising flour

1¾ oz dark chocolate

SYRUP

½ cup sugar

6 tbsp water

3 tbsp brandy or sherry

TO DECORATE

1¾ cup heavy cream

3

5

1 Grease a 9-inch ring pan. To make the triangles, place a sheet of baking parchment on to a cookie sheet and place alternate spoonfuls of the dark and white chocolate on to the parchment. Spread together to form a thick marbled layer; Let it set. Cut into squares, then into triangles.

2 To make the cake, beat the margarine and sugar until light and fluffy. Beat in the vanilla extract. Gradually add the eggs, beating well after each addition. Fold in the flour. Divide the mixture in half. Melt the dark chocolate and stir into one half.

3 Place spoonfuls of each mixture into the prepared pan and swirl together with a skewer to create a marbled effect.

4 Bake in a preheated oven, 375°F, for 30 minutes, or until the cake is springy to the touch. Let it cool in the pan for a few minutes, then transfer to a wire rack to cool completely.

5 To make the syrup, place the sugar in a small pan with the water and heat until the sugar has dissolved. Boil for 1–2 minutes. Remove from the heat and stir in the brandy or sherry. Let the syrup cool slightly, then spoon it slowly over the cake, letting it soak into the sponge. Whip the cream and pipe swirls of it on top of the cake. Decorate with the chocolate triangles.

yogurt & pineapple cake

Decorated with thick yogurt and canned pineapple, this is a
low-fat cake, but it is by no means lacking in flavor.

2

Serves 9

¼ cup low-fat spread

4½ oz superfine sugar

¾ cup self-rising flour, sifted

3 tbsp unsweetened cocoa, sifted

1½ tsp baking powder

2 eggs

8 oz canned pineapple pieces in
   unsweetened juice

½ cup low-fat thick unsweetened yogurt

about 1 tbsp confectioners' sugar

grated chocolate, to decorate

3

1 Lightly grease an 8-inch square
  cake pan.

2 Place the low-fat spread, superfine
  sugar, flour, unsweetened cocoa,
baking powder, and eggs in a large
mixing bowl. Beat with a wooden spoon
or electric hand whisk until smooth.

3 Pour the cake mixture into the
  prepared pan and level the surface.
Bake it in a preheated oven, 325°F, for
20–25 minutes, or until springy to the
touch. Let the cake cool slightly in the
pan before transferring to a wire rack to
cool completely.

4 Drain the pineapple, then chop the
  pieces and drain again. Reserve a
little pineapple for decoration, then stir
the rest into the yogurt and sweeten to
taste with confectioners' sugar.

4

5 Spread the pineapple and yogurt
  mixture over the cake and decorate
with the reserved pineapple pieces.
Sprinkle with the grated chocolate.

cook's tip

Store the cake, undecorated,
in an airtight container for
up to 3 days. Once decorated,
refrigerate and use within
2 days.

dairy free sponge

This is a healthy variation of the classic sponge layer cake
and is suitable for vegans.

3

Makes an 8-inch cake

1¾ cups self-rising whole-wheat flour

2 tsp baking powder

¼ cup superfine sugar

6 tbsp sunflower oil

1 cup water

1 tsp vanilla extract

4 tbsp strawberry or raspberry reduced-
    sugar spread

superfine sugar, for dusting

3

4

variation

Use melted vegan butter or margarine instead of the sunflower oil if you prefer, but let it cool before adding it to the dry ingredients in step 3.

1 Grease two 8-inch sandwich layer pans and line them smoothly with baking parchment.

2 Sift the flour and baking powder into a large mixing bowl, stirring in any bran remaining in the sifter. Stir in the superfine sugar.

3 Pour in the sunflower oil, water, and vanilla extract and mix well with a wooden spoon for about 1 minute, or until the cake mixture reaches a smooth consistency.

4 Divide the mixture between the prepared pans.

5 Bake in a preheated oven, 350°F, for about 25–30 minutes, or until the center springs back when lightly touched. Let cool in the pans before turning out and transferring to a wire rack.

6 To serve, remove the baking parchment and place one of the sponges on to a serving plate. Spread with the jam and place the other sponge on top. Dust with a little superfine sugar.

fluted orange cake

Baking in a deep, fluted kugelhopf pan ensures that you create a cake with a stunning shape. The moist cake is full of fresh orange flavor.

3

Serves 6-8

1 cup butter, softened

1 cup superfine sugar

4 eggs, separated

3¾ cups all-purpose flour

pinch of salt

3 tsp baking powder

1¼ cups fresh orange juice

1 tbsp orange flower water

1 tsp grated orange rind

SYRUP

¾ cup orange juice

1 cup granulated sugar

7

1 Grease and flour a 10-inch kugelhopf pan or deep ring mold.

2 In a bowl, cream together the butter and superfine sugar until light and fluffy. Add the egg yolks one at a time, whisking well after each addition.

3 Sift together the flour, salt, and baking powder into a separate bowl. Fold the dry ingredients and the orange juice alternately into the creamed mixture with a metal spoon, working as lightly as possible. Stir in the orange flower water and orange rind.

4 Whisk the egg whites until they reach the soft peak stage and fold them into the mixture.

5 Pour into the prepared mold and bake in a preheated oven, 350°F, for 50–55 minutes, or until a metal skewer inserted into the center of the cake comes out clean.

6 In a saucepan, bring the orange juice and sugar to a boil, then simmer for 5 minutes until the sugar has dissolved.

7 Remove the cake from the oven and let cool in the pan for 10 minutes. Prick the top of the cake with a fine skewer and brush over half of the syrup. Let the cake cool for another 10 minutes. Invert the cake on to a wire rack placed over a deep plate and brush the syrup over the cake until it is entirely covered. Serve immediately.

sugarless gem cake

This cake is full of flavor from the mixed fruits. The fruit gives the cake its sweetness, so there is no need for extra sugar.

Serves 8-10

3 cups all-purpose flour

2 tsp baking powder

1 tsp ground allspice

½ cup butter, cut into small pieces

2¾ oz ready-to-eat dried apricots, chopped

2¾ oz dates, chopped

⅓ cup candied cherries, chopped

¾ cup raisins

½ cup milk

2 eggs, beaten

grated rind of 1 orange

5–6 tbsp orange juice

3 tbsp liquid honey

1 Grease an 8-inch round cake pan and line the bottom with baking parchment.

3

2 Sift together the flour, baking powder, and ground allspice into a large mixing bowl.

3 Rub in the butter with your fingers until the mixture resembles fine bread crumbs.

4

4 Carefully stir in the apricots, dates, candied cherries, and raisins with the milk, beaten eggs, grated orange rind, and orange juice.

5 Stir in the honey and mix everything together to form a soft dropping consistency. Spoon into the prepared cake pan and level the surface.

6 Bake in a preheated oven, 350°F, for 1 hour, or until a fine skewer inserted into the center of the cake comes out clean.

7 Let the cake cool in the pan before turning out.

5

chocolate & raspberry layer cake

Adding yogurt to the cake mixture gives this baked cake a deliciously moist texture.

Serves 8-10

⅔ cup vegetable oil

⅔ cup whole-milk unsweetened yogurt

1¼ cups light muscovado sugar

3 eggs, beaten

¼ cup whole-wheat self-rising flour

1 cup self-rising flour, sifted

2 tbsp unsweetened cocoa

1 tsp baking soda

1¼ oz dark chocolate, melted

FILLING AND TOPPING

⅔ cup whole-milk unsweetened yogurt

⅔ cup heavy cream

8 oz fresh soft fruit, such as strawberries or raspberries

2

3

5

1 Grease a deep 9-inch round cake pan and line the bottom with baking parchment.

2 Place the oil, yogurt, sugar, and beaten eggs in a large mixing bowl and beat together until well combined. Sift together the flours, unsweetened cocoa, and baking soda together and beat into the bowl until well combined. Beat in the melted chocolate.

3 Pour into the prepared pan and bake in a preheated oven, 350°F, for 45–50 minutes, or until a fine skewer inserted into the center comes out clean. Let cool in the pan for 5 minutes, then turn out on to a wire rack to cool completely. When cold, split the cake into 3 layers.

4 To make the filling, place the yogurt and cream in a large mixing bowl and whisk well until the mixture stands in soft peaks.

5 Place one layer of cake on to a serving plate and spread with some of the cream. Top with a little of the fruit (slicing larger fruit such as strawberries). Repeat with the next layer. Top with the final layer of cake and spread with the rest of the cream. Arrange more fruit on top and cut the cake into wedges to serve.

chocolate cake with citrus frosting

This is a classic, consisting of a rich, melt-in-the-mouth, chocolate cake with a citrus-flavored frosting.

4

Serves 8

3¼ oz dark chocolate

2¼ cups self-rising flour

1 tsp baking soda

1 cup butter

2½ cups dark muscovado sugar

1 tsp vanilla extract

3 eggs

½ cup buttermilk

2 cups boiling water

FROSTING

1¼ cups superfine sugar

2 egg whites

1 tbsp lemon juice

3 tbsp orange juice

candied orange peel, to decorate

5

6

3 Fold the melted chocolate into the mixture until well blended. Gradually fold in the remaining flour, then stir in the buttermilk and boiling water.

4 Divide the mixture between the pans and level the tops. Bake in a preheated oven, 375°F, for 30 minutes, or until springy to the touch. Let cool in the pan for 5 minutes, then transfer to a wire rack to cool completely.

5 Place the frosting ingredients in a large bowl set over a pan of gently simmering water. Whisk, preferably with an electric beater, until thickened and forming soft peaks. Remove from the heat and whisk until the mixture is cool.

6 Sandwich the 2 cakes together with a little of the frosting, then spread the remainder over the sides and top of the cake, swirling it as you do so. Decorate with the candied orange peel.

1 Lightly grease two 8-inch shallow round cake pans and line the bottoms. Melt the chocolate in a pan. Sift together the flour and baking soda.

2 Beat the butter and sugar in a bowl until pale and fluffy. Beat in the vanilla extract and the eggs, one at a time and beating well after each addition. Add a little flour if the mixture begins to curdle.

sandwich cake with chocolate topping

A simple-to-make family cake, ideal for an everyday treat. Keep the decoration as simple as you like—you could use a ready-made frosting or filling, if desired.

2

3

4

Serves 8-10

½ cup soft margarine

½ cup superfine sugar

2 eggs

1 tbsp light corn syrup

1 cup self-rising flour, sifted

2 tbsp unsweetened cocoa, sifted

FILLING AND TOPPING

¼ cup confectioners' sugar, sifted

2 tbsp butter

3½ oz white or milk cooking chocolate

a little milk or white chocolate, melted

　(optional)

cook's tip

Ensure that you eat this cake on the day of baking, as it does not keep well.

1 Lightly grease two 7-inch shallow cake pans.

2 Place all of the ingredients for the cake in a large mixing bowl and beat with a wooden spoon or electric hand whisk to form a smooth mixture.

3 Divide the mixture between the prepared pans and level the tops. Bake in a preheated oven, 325°F, for 20 minutes, or until springy to the touch. Cool for a few minutes in the pans before transferring to a wire rack to cool completely.

4 To make the filling, beat the confectioners' sugar and butter together in a bowl until light and fluffy. Melt the cooking chocolate and beat half into the frosting mixture. Use the filling to sandwich the 2 cakes together.

5 Spread the remaining melted cooking chocolate over the top of the cake. Pipe circles of contrasting melted milk or white chocolate and then feather them into the cooking chocolate with a toothpick, if desired. Let it set before serving.

chocolate vacherin with raspberries & cream

A vacherin is made of layers of crisp meringue sandwiched together with fruit and cream. It is marvelous for special occasions.

Serves 10-12

3 egg whites

¾ cup superfine sugar

1 tsp cornstarch

1 oz dark chocolate, grated

FILLING

6 oz dark chocolate

2 cups heavy cream, whipped

12 oz fresh raspberries

a little melted chocolate, to decorate

1 Draw 3 rectangles, 10 x 4 inches, on sheets of baking parchment and place them on 2 cookie sheets.

2 Whisk the egg whites in a mixing bowl until standing in soft peaks, then gradually whisk in half of the sugar and continue whisking until the mixture is very stiff and glossy.

3 Carefully fold in the rest of the sugar, the cornstarch, and the grated dark chocolate with a metal spoon or a spatula.

1

6

4 Spoon the meringue mixture into a pastry bag fitted with a ½-inch/1-cm plain tip and pipe lines across each of the rectangles.

5 Bake in a preheated oven, 275°F, for 1½ hours, changing the positions of the cookie sheets halfway through. Without opening the oven door, turn off the oven and let the meringues cool in the oven, then peel away the parchment.

4

6 For the filling, melt the chocolate and spread it over 2 of the meringue layers. Let the filling harden.

7 To assemble the vacherin, place 1 chocolate-coated meringue on a plate and top with about one-third of the cream and raspberries. Gently place the second chocolate-coated meringue on top and spread with half of the remaining cream and raspberries.

8 Place the last meringue on the top and decorate it with the remaining cream and raspberries. Drizzle a little melted chocolate over the top and serve.

white chocolate & apricot squares

The white chocolate makes this a very rich cake, so serve it cut into small bars or squares or sliced thinly.

Makes 12 bars

½ cup butter

6 oz white chocolate, chopped

4 eggs

½ cup superfine sugar

1¾ cups all-purpose flour, sifted

1 tsp baking powder

pinch of salt

3½ oz ready-to-eat dried apricots, chopped

variation

Replace the white chocolate with milk or dark chocolate, if you prefer.

2

3

3 Beat the eggs and superfine sugar into the butter and chocolate mixture until well combined.

4 Fold in the flour, baking powder, salt, and chopped dried apricots and mix well.

5 Pour the mixture into the pan and bake in a preheated oven, 350°F, for 25–30 minutes.

6 The center of the cake may not be completely firm, but it will set as it cools. Leave in the pan to cool.

7 When the cake is completely cold turn it out and slice into bars or squares.

4

1 Lightly grease a 9-inch square cake pan and line the base smoothly with a sheet of baking parchment.

2 Melt the butter and chocolate in a heatproof bowl set over a saucepan of simmering water. Stir frequently with a wooden spoon until the mixture is mooth and glossy. Leave the mixture to cool.

butter cream log

This unusual cake is very popular with children, who love
the appearance of the layers when it is sliced.

Serves 8-10

¼ cup soft margarine

½ cup superfine sugar

2 eggs

¼ cup self-rising flour

¼ cup unsweetened cocoa

2 tbsp milk

WHITE CHOCOLATE BUTTER CREAM

2¼ oz white chocolate

2 tbsp milk

½ cup butter

¼ cup confectioners' sugar

2 tbsp orange-flavored liqueur

large dark chocolate curls (see page 50), to
  decorate

1 Grease and line the sides of two
14-oz food cans.

2 Beat together the margarine and
sugar in a bowl until light and fluffy.
Gradually add the eggs, beating well
after each addition. Sift together the flour
and unsweetened cocoa and fold into
the cake mixture. Fold in the milk.

3 Divide the mixture between the two
prepared cans. Stand the cans on
a cookie sheet and bake in a preheated
oven, 350°F, for about 40 minutes, or
until springy to the touch. Let cool for
about 5 minutes in the cans, then turn
out and let cool completely on a wire
rack.

1

3

5

4 To make the butter cream,
put the chocolate and milk
in a pan and heat gently until the
chocolate has melted, stirring
until well combined. Let cool slightly.
Beat together the butter and
confectioners' sugar until light and fluffy.
Beat in the orange liqueur. Gradually beat
in the chocolate mixture.

5 To assemble the log, cut both
cakes into ½-inch thick slices, then
reassemble them by sandwiching the
slices together with some of the butter
cream.

6 Place the cake on a serving plate
and spread the remaining butter
cream over the top and sides. Decorate
with the chocolate curls, then serve the
cake cut diagonally into slices.

marbled chocolate loaf

An old-fashioned favorite, this cake will keep well if stored
in an airtight container or wrapped in foil in a cool place.

4

5

Serves 10

¼ cup superfine sugar

¼ cup soft margarine

½ tsp vanilla extract

3 eggs

2 cups self-rising flour, sifted

1¼ oz dark chocolate

confectioners' sugar, to dust

1 Lightly grease a 1-lb loaf pan.

2 Beat together the sugar and soft
margarine in a large mixing bowl until
light and fluffy.

3 Beat in the vanilla extract. Gradually
add the eggs, beating well after
each addition. Carefully fold in the self-
rising flour.

4 Divide the mixture in half. Melt the
dark chocolate and stir into one half
of the mixture until well combined.

5 Place the vanilla mixture in the pan
and level the top. Spread the
chocolate layer over the vanilla layer.

6 Bake in a preheated oven, 375°F,
for 30 minutes, or until springy to
the touch.

8

7 Let cool in the pan before
transferring the loaf to a wire rack to
cool completely.

8 Serve the cake dusted with
confectioners' sugar.

yule log

This is a traditional French Christmas cake. It consists of a chocolate cake filled and encased in a delicious rich chocolate frosting.

1

Serves 8-10

CAKE

4 eggs

7 tbsp superfine sugar

⅔ cup self-rising flour

2 tbsp unsweetened cocoa

FROSTING

5½ oz dark chocolate

2 egg yolks

⅔ cup milk

½ cup butter

4 tbsp confectioners' sugar

2 tbsp rum (optional)

TO DECORATE

a little white glacé or royal frosting

confectioners' sugar, to dust

holly or seasonal cake decorations

2

 Grease and line a 12 x 9-inch Bundt pan. Whisk the eggs and superfine sugar in a bowl with electric beaters for 10 minutes, or until the mixture is very light and foamy and the whisk leaves a trail. Sift the flour and unsweetened cocoa and fold in. Pour into the prepared pan and bake in a preheated oven, 400°F, for 12 minutes, or until springy to the touch. Turn out on to a piece of baking parchment which has been sprinkled with a little superfine sugar. Peel off the lining parchment and trim the edges. Cut a small slit halfway into the cake about ½-inch from one short end. Starting at that end, roll up tightly, enclosing the parchment. Place on a wire rack to cool.

2

2 To make the frosting, break the chocolate into pieces and melt it over a pan of hot water. Beat in the egg yolks, then whisk in the milk and cook until the mixture thickens enough to coat the back of a wooden spoon, stirring. Cover with dampened waxed paper and cool. Beat the butter and sugar until pale and fluffy. Beat in the custard and rum, if using. Unroll the sponge, then spread with one-third of the frosting and roll up again. Place on a serving plate. Spread the remaining frosting over the cake and mark with a fork to give the effect of bark. Let it set. Pipe white frosting to form the rings of the log. Sprinkle with sugar and decorate.

apple & raspberry cake

This can be eaten as a cake at tea time or with a cup of coffee, or it can be warmed through and served with cream for a dessert.

Makes an 8-inch cake

2 cups self-rising flour

1 tsp baking powder

⅓ cup butter, cut into small pieces

⅓ cup superfine sugar

1¾ oz dried apple, chopped

5 tbsp raisins

⅔ cup hard cider

1 egg, beaten

6 oz raspberries

variation

If you don't want to use cider, replace it with clear apple juice.

3

4

4

1 Grease an 8-inch cake pan and line it with baking parchment.

2 Sift the flour and baking powder into a mixing bowl and rub in the butter with your fingers until the mixture resembles fine bread crumbs.

3 Stir in the superfine sugar, chopped dried apple, and raisins.

4 Pour in the sweet cider and egg and mix together until thoroughly blended. Stir in the raspberries very gently so they do not break up.

5 Pour the mixture into the prepared cake pan.

6 Bake in a preheated oven, 375°F, for about 40 minutes, or until risen and lightly golden.

7 Let the cake cool in the pan, then turn out on to a wire rack. Let stand until completely cold before serving.

spiced apple cream shortcakes

This traditional American dessert is a freshly baked sweet biscuit, split and filled with sliced apples and whipped cream. Eat these shortcakes warm or cold.

3

Serves 8

1¼ cups all-purpose flour

½ tsp salt

1 tsp baking powder

1 tbsp superfine sugar

1 tbsp butter, cut into
    small pieces

¼ cup milk

confectioners' sugar, for dusting

FILLING

3 eating apples, peeled, cored,
    and sliced

½ cup superfine sugar

1 tbsp lemon juice

1 tsp ground cinnamon

1½ cups water

½ cup heavy cream, lightly whipped

6

1 Lightly grease a cookie sheet.

2 Sift together the flour, salt, and baking powder into a mixing bowl. Stir in the sugar, then rub in the butter with your fingertips until the mixture resembles fine bread crumbs.

3 Pour in the milk and mix everything to a soft dough. On a lightly floured counter, knead the dough lightly, then roll out to a thickness of ½ inch. Stamp out 4 rounds, using a 2-inch cutter. Transfer the rounds to the prepared cookie sheet.

4 Bake in a preheated oven at 425°F, for about 15 minutes, or until the shortcakes are well risen and lightly browned. Let cool while you make the apple filling.

5 To make the filling, place the apple slices, sugar, lemon juice, and cinnamon in a pan.

6 Add the water and bring to a boil, then simmer uncovered for 5–10 minutes, or until the apples are tender. Cool a little, then remove the apples from the pan.

7 To serve, split the shortcakes in half. Place each bottom half on an individual serving plate and spoon on one fourth of the apple slices, then the cream. Place the other half of the shortcake on top. Serve dusted with confectioners' sugar, if desired.

coconut & raspberry roulade

This coconut-flavored roulade is encased in a rich chocolate coating. A fresh raspberry coulis gives a lovely fresh contrast to the sweetness of the roulade.

Serves 8-10

3 eggs

¼ cup superfine sugar

½ cup self-rising flour

1 tbsp block creamed coconut, softened
    with 1 tbsp boiling water

1 oz shredded coconut

6 tbsp good raspberry conserve

CHOCOLATE COATING

7 oz dark chocolate

¼ cup butter

2 tbsp light corn syrup

RASPBERRY COULIS

8 oz fresh or frozen raspberries,
    thawed if frozen

2 tbsp water

4 tbsp confectioners' sugar

1 Grease and line a 12 x 9-inch Bundt pan. Whisk the eggs and superfine sugar in a large mixing bowl with electric beaters for about 10 minutes, or until the mixture is very light and foamy and the whisk leaves a trail that lasts a few seconds when lifted.

2 Sift the flour and fold in with a metal spoon or a spatula. Fold in the creamed coconut and shredded coconut. Pour into the prepared pan and bake in a preheated oven, 400°F, for 10–12 minutes, or until springy to the touch.

2

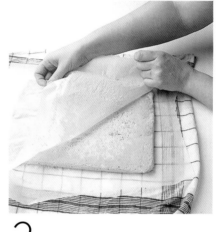

3

3 Sprinkle a sheet of baking parchment with a little superfine sugar and place on top of a cloth. Turn the cake out on to the parchment and carefully peel away the lining parchment. Spread the conserve over the sponge and roll up from the short end, using the tea towel to help you. Place seam-side down on a wire rack and let cool completely.

4 To make the coating, melt the chocolate and butter, stirring. Stir in the light corn syrup; let cool for 5 minutes. Spread it over the roulade and let it set. To make the coulis, purée the fruit in a food processor with the water and sugar; sift to remove the seeds. Cut the roulade into slices and serve with the coulis.

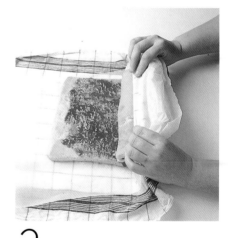

3

creamy chocolate & raspberry roulade

Don't worry if this cake cracks when rolled—this is quite normal. If it doesn't crack, you can consider yourself a real chocolate wizard in the kitchen!

4

Serves 6-8

2 tbsp water

6 eggs

¾ cup superfine sugar

¼ cup all-purpose flour

1 tbsp unsweetened cocoa

FILLING

1¼ cups heavy cream

2¾ oz sliced strawberries

TO DECORATE

confectioners' sugar

chocolate leaves (see below)

5

1 Line a 15 x 10-inch pan. Melt the chocolate in the water, stirring. Let cool slightly.

2 Place the eggs and sugar in a bowl and whisk for 10 minutes, or until the mixture is pale and foamy and the whisk leaves a trail when lifted. Whisk in the chocolate in a thin stream. Sift together the flour and unsweetened cocoa and fold into the mixture. Pour into the pan; level the top.

3 Bake in a preheated oven, 400°F, for 12 minutes. Dust a sheet of baking parchment with a little confectioners' sugar. Turn out the roulade and remove the lining parchment. Roll up the roulade with the fresh parchment inside. Place on a wire rack, then cover with a damp dish towel and let cool.

5

4 Whisk the cream until just holding its shape. Unroll the roulade and scatter over the fruit. Spread three-fourths of the cream over the roulade and re-roll. Dust with confectioners' sugar. Place the roulade on a plate. Pipe the rest of the cream down the center and decorate with chocolate leaves.

5 To make chocolate leaves, wash some rose, holly, or ivy leaves and pat dry. Melt some chocolate and brush over the leaves. Set aside to harden. Repeat with 2–3 layers of chocolate. Carefully peel the leaves away from the chocolate.

This chapter contains a delicious array of small cakes, and you are sure to be tempted by our wonderful selection of cookies and tarts. Make any day special with a home-made meringue or brownie, or a chocolate cookie to be served with coffee, as a snack or to accompany a special dessert. Although some take a little longer to make, most are quick and easy to prepare and decoration is often simple, although you can get carried away if you like!

You'll find recipes for old favorites as well as some exciting new creations to tickle your taste-buds. So whether you are looking for a quick, easy recipe for a snack-time treat, or a selection of mouthwatering treats to offer guests, there will be something here to tempt even the strongest-willed adult or the fussiest child.

small cakes, cookies & tarts

lemon cream butterflies

Filled with a tangy lemon cream, these appealing cakes will be a favorite with adults and children alike.

Makes 12

½ cup soft margarine

½ cup superfine sugar

1¼ cups self-rising flour

2 large eggs

2 tbsp unsweetened cocoa

1 oz dark chocolate, melted

LEMON BUTTER CREAM

generous ⅓ cup unsalted butter, softened

1¼ cups confectioners' sugar, sifted

grated rind of ½ lemon

1 tbsp lemon juice

confectioners' sugar, to dust

variation

For a chocolate butter cream, beat the butter and confectioners' sugar together, then beat in 1 oz melted dark chocolate.

1

2

1 Place 12 parchment shells in a muffin pan. Place all of the ingredients for the cakes, except for the melted chocolate, in a large mixing bowl and beat with electric beaters until the mixture is just smooth. Beat in the chocolate.

2 Spoon equal amounts of the cake mixture into each parchment shell, filling them three-fourths full. Bake in a preheated oven, 350°F, for 15 minutes, or until springy to the touch. Transfer the cakes to a wire rack and let cool.

3 To make the lemon butter cream, place the butter in a mixing bowl and beat until fluffy, then gradually beat in the confectioners' sugar. Beat in the lemon rind and gradually add the lemon juice, beating well.

4

4 When cold, cut the top off each cake, using a serrated knife. Cut each top in half.

5 Spread or pipe the butter cream frosting over the cut surface of each cake and push the 2 cut pieces of cake top into the frosting to form wings. Sprinkle with confectioners' sugar.

refrigerator squares

These are handy little squares to keep in the refrigerator for when unexpected guests arrive. Children will also enjoy making them.

1

Makes 16

9¾ oz dark chocolate

¼ cup butter

4 tbsp light corn syrup

2 tbsp dark rum (optional)

6 oz plain cookies

1 oz toasted rice cereal

¼ cup chopped walnuts or

    pecan nuts

¼ cup candied cherries, coarsely chopped

1 oz white chocolate, to decorate

2

1 Place the dark chocolate in a large mixing bowl with the butter, syrup, and rum, if using, and set over a pan of gently simmering water until melted, stirring until blended.

2 Break the cookies into small pieces and stir into the chocolate mixture along with the rice cereal, nuts, and candied cherries.

3 Line a 7-inch square cake pan with baking parchment. Pour the mixture into the pan and level the top, pressing down well with the back of a spoon. Chill for 2 hours.

4 To decorate, melt the white chocolate and drizzle it over the top of the cake in a random pattern. Let it set. To serve, carefully turn out of the pan and remove the baking parchment. Cut into 16 squares.

4

variation

Brandy or an orange-flavored liqueur can be used instead of the rum, if you prefer. Cherry brandy also works well.

variation

For a coconut flavor, replace the rice cereal with shredded coconut and add a coconut-flavored liqueur.

sunflower seed cakes

These are moist, cakelike squares with a lovely spicy flavor.

Makes 12

1 cup butter, softened

1¼ cups superfine sugar

3 eggs, beaten

2 cups self-raising flour

⅟ tsp baking soda

1 tbsp ground cinnamon

⅟ cup sour cream

3⅟ oz sunflower seeds

1 Grease a 9-inch square cake pan and line the base with baking parchment.

2 In a large mixing bowl, cream together the butter and superfine sugar until the mixture is light and fluffy.

3 Gradually add the beaten eggs to the mixture, beating thoroughly after each addition.

3

4

4 Sift the self-raising flour, baking soda, and ground cinnamon into the creamed mixture and fold in gently, using a metal spoon.

5 Spoon in the sour cream and sunflower seeds and gently mix until well combined.

6 Spoon the mixture into the prepared cake pan and level the surface with the back of a spoon or a knife.

7 Bake in a preheated oven, 350°F, for about 45 minutes, or until the mixture is firm to the touch when pressed with a finger.

8 Loosen the edges with a round-bladed knife, then turn out on to a wire rack to cool completely. Slice into 12 squares.

5

cook's tip

These moist squares will freeze well and will keep for up to 1 month.

mini meringues

These are just as meringues should be—as light as air and at the same time crisp and melt-in-the-mouth.

2

Makes about 13

4 egg whites

pinch of salt

½ cup granulated sugar

½ cup superfine sugar

1¼ cups heavy cream, whipped lightly

5

variation

For a finer texture, replace the granulated sugar with superfine sugar.

1 Carefully line 3 cookie sheets with sheets of baking parchment.

2 In a large clean bowl, whisk together the egg whites and salt until they are stiff, using an electric hand-held whisk or a balloon whisk. (You should be able to turn the bowl upside down without any movement from the egg whites.)

3 Whisk in the granulated sugar a little at a time; at this stage, the meringue should be starting to look glossy.

4 Sprinkle in the superfine sugar a little at a time and continue whisking until all the sugar has been incorporated and the meringue is thick and white and stands in tall peaks.

5 Transfer the meringue mixture to a pastry bag fitted with a ¾-inch star tip. Pipe about 26 small whirls on to the prepared cookie sheets.

6 Bake in a preheated oven, 250°F, for 1½ hours, or until the meringues are pale golden in color and can be easily lifted off the parchment. Let them cool in the turned-off oven overnight.

7 Just before serving, sandwich the meringues together in pairs with the cream and arrange on a serving plate.

chocolate caramel squares

These rich squares of shortbread are topped with caramel and finished with chocolate to make a very special treat!

Makes 12 bars

1¼ cups all-purpose flour

¼ cup butter, cut into small pieces

3 tbsp soft brown sugar, sifted

TOPPING

10 tsp butter

3 tbsp soft brown sugar

14 oz canned condensed milk

5½ oz milk chocolate

1 Grease a 9-inch square cake pan.

2 Sift the flour into a mixing bowl and rub in the butter with your fingers until the mixture resembles fine bread crumbs. Add the sugar and mix to form a firm dough.

2

3 Press the dough into the bottom of the prepared pan and prick all over with a fork.

3

4 Bake in a preheated oven, 375°F, for 20 minutes, or until lightly golden. Let cool in the pan.

5 To make the topping, place the butter, sugar, and condensed milk in a non-stick pan and cook over a gentle heat, stirring constantly, until the mixture comes to a boil.

6 Reduce the heat and cook for 4–5 minutes until the caramel is pale golden and thick and is coming away from the sides of the pan. Pour the topping over the shortbread base and let cool.

6

7 When the caramel topping is firm, melt the milk chocolate in a heatproof bowl set over a pan of simmering water. Spread the melted chocolate over the topping, let it set in a cool place, then cut the shortbread into squares or fingers to serve.

cook's tip

Ensure the caramel layer is completely cool and set before coating it with the melted chocolate, otherwise they will mix together.

chocolate & pistachio brownies

Choose a good-quality chocolate for these brownies
to give them a rich flavor that is not too sweet.

4 4 4

Makes 12

5½ oz dark chocolate, broken into pieces

1 cup butter, softened

2 cups self-rising flour

½ cup superfine sugar

4 eggs, beaten

2¼ oz pistachio nuts, chopped

3½ oz white chocolate,
    coarsely chopped

confectioners' sugar, for dusting

1 Lightly grease a 9-inch baking pan
and line with waxed paper.

2 Melt the dark chocolate and butter in
a heatproof bowl set over a pan of
simmering water. Let cool slightly.

3 Sift the flour into a separate mixing
bowl and stir in the superfine sugar.

4 Stir the eggs into the melted
chocolate mixture, then pour this
mixture into the flour and sugar mixture,
beating well. Stir in the pistachio nuts
and white chocolate, then pour the
mixture into the pan, spreading it evenly
into the corners.

5 Bake in a preheated oven, 350°F, for
30–35 minutes, or until firm to the
touch. Let cool in the pan for 20 minutes,
then turn out on to a wire rack.

6 Dust the brownie with confectioners'
sugar and then cut into 12 pieces
when cold.

cook's tip

The brownie won't be
completely firm in the middle
when it is removed from the
oven, but it will set when it
has cooled.

chocolate rice squares

A favorite with children, this version of crispy bites has been
given a new twist that is sure to be popular.

cook's tip

These bites can be made up to 4 days ahead. Keep them covered in the refrigerator until ready to use.

3

6

7

Makes 16

WHITE LAYER

4 tbsp butter

1 tbsp light corn syrup

5½ oz white chocolate

1¾ oz toasted rice cereal

DARK LAYER

4 tbsp butter

2 tbsp light corn syrup

dark chocolate, broken into small pieces

2¾ oz toasted rice cereal

5 To make the dark chocolate layer, melt the butter, light corn syrup, and dark chocolate in a bowl set over a pan of gently simmering water.

6 Remove from the heat and stir in the rice cereal until it is well coated. Pour the dark chocolate layer over the hardened white chocolate layer and chill until the top layer has hardened.

7 Turn out of the cake pan and then cut into 16 small squares, using a sharp knife.

1 Grease an 8-inch square cake pan and line with baking parchment.

2 To make the white chocolate layer, melt the butter, light corn syrup, and chocolate in a bowl set over a pan of gently simmering water.

3 Remove from the heat and stir in the rice cereal until it is well combined .

4 Press into the prepared pan and level the surface.

frosted chocolate & cream cheese brownies

This traditional brownie mixture has a cream cheese ribbon through the center and is topped with a delicious chocolate fudge frosting.

Makes 16

7 oz low-fat soft cheese

½ tsp vanilla extract

generous 1 cup superfine sugar

2 eggs

generous ⅛ cup butter

3 tbsp unsweetened cocoa

¾ cup self-rising flour, sifted

1¾ oz pecans, chopped

FUDGE FROSTING

1 tbsp butter

1 tbsp milk

½ cup confectioners' sugar

2 tbsp unsweetened cocoa

pecans, to decorate (optional)

2

3

4

1 Lightly grease an 8-inch square shallow cake pan and line the bottom.

variation

Omit the cheese layer if preferred. Use walnuts in place of the pecans.

2 Beat together the cheese, vanilla extract, and 5 tsp of the superfine sugar until smooth, then set aside.

3 Beat the eggs and remaining superfine sugar together until light and fluffy. Place the butter and unsweetened cocoa in a small pan and heat gently, stirring until the butter melts

and the mixture combines, then stir it into the egg mixture. Fold in the flour and nuts.

4 Pour half of the brownie mixture into the pan and level the top. Carefully spread the soft cheese over it, then cover it with the remaining brownie mixture. Bake in a preheated oven, 350°F, for 40–45 minutes. Cool in the pan.

5 To make the frosting, melt the butter in the milk. Stir in the confectioners' sugar and unsweetened cocoa. Spread the frosting over the brownies and decorate with pecans, if using. Let the frosting set, then cut into squares to serve.

sweet hazelnut pastries

These delicious chocolate and hazelnut cookies are very simple to make, yet so effective. For very young children, leave out the chopped nuts.

Makes about 26

13 oz ready-made puff pastry

8 tbsp chocolate hazelnut spread

⅓ cup chopped toasted hazelnuts

5 tsp superfine sugar

2

3

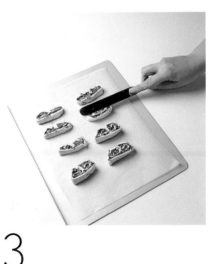

3

1 Lightly grease a cookie sheet. On a
lightly floured counter, roll out the
puff pastry to a rectangle about
15 x 9 inches in size.

2 Spread the chocolate hazelnut
spread over the pastry using a
spatula, then scatter the chopped
hazelnuts over the top.

3 Roll up one long side of the pastry to
the center, then roll up the other side
so that they meet in the center. Where
the pieces meet, dampen the edges with
a little water to join them. Using a sharp
knife, cut into thin slices. Place each slice
on to the prepared baking sheet and
flatten slightly with a spatula. Sprinkle the
slices with the superfine sugar.

4 Bake in a preheated oven, 425°F, for
about 10–15 minutes, or until
golden. Transfer to a wire rack to cool.

white chocolate cakes

A variation on an old favorite, both kids and grown-ups will love these sumptuous little cakes.

Makes 18

generous ½ cup butter, softened

7 tbsp superfine sugar

2 eggs, lightly beaten

1¼ cups self-rising flour

2 tbsp milk

⅓ cup dark chocolate chips

¼ cup unsweetened cocoa

FROSTING

8 oz white chocolate

5½ oz low-fat soft cheese

variation

Add white chocolate chips or chopped pecan nuts to the mixture instead of the dark chocolate chips, if you prefer. You can also add the finely grated rind of 1 orange for a chocolate and orange flavor.

2

2

3

1 Line an 18-hole muffin pan with individual parchment shells.

2 Beat together the butter and sugar until pale and fluffy. Gradually add the eggs, beating well after each addition. Add a little of the flour if the mixture begins to curdle. Add the milk, then fold in the chocolate chips.

3 Sift together the flour and unsweetened cocoa and fold into the mixture with a metal spoon or spatula. Divide the mixture equally between the paper shells and level the tops.

4 Bake in a preheated oven, 350°F, for 20 minutes, or until well risen and springy to the touch. Let cool on a wire rack.

5 To make the frosting, melt the chocolate, then let cool slightly. Beat the cream cheese until softened slightly, then beat in the melted chocolate. Spread a little of the frosting over each cake and chill for 1 hour before serving.

dark chocolate brownies

Everyone loves chocolate brownies and these are so gooey
and delicious they are impossible to resist!

2

Makes 9

generous ½ cup unsalted butter

¼ cup superfine sugar

½ cup dark brown sugar

4½ oz dark chocolate

1 tbsp light corn syrup

2 eggs

1 tsp chocolate or vanilla extract

¼ cup all-purpose flour

2 tbsp unsweetened cocoa

½ tsp baking powder

3

4

1 Lightly grease an 8-inch shallow
square cake pan and line the
bottom.

2 Place the butter, sugars, dark
chocolate, and light corn syrup in a
heavy-bottomed pan and heat gently,
stirring until the mixture is well blended
and smooth. Remove from the heat and
let cool.

3 Beat together the eggs and extract.
Whisk in the cooled chocolate
mixture.

4 Sift together the flour, unsweetened
cocoa, and baking powder and fold
carefully into the egg and chocolate
mixture, using a metal spoon or a
spatula.

5 Spoon the mixture into the prepared
pan and bake in a preheated oven,
350°F, for 25 minutes, or until the top is
crisp and the edge of the cake is
beginning to shrink away from the pan.
The inside of the cake mixture will still be
quite stodgy and soft to the touch.

6 Let the cake cool completely in
the pan, then cut it into squares
to serve.

cook's tip

This cake can be well wrapped
and frozen for up to 2 months.
Defrost at room temperature
for about 2 hours or overnight
in the refrigerator.

chewy vanilla coconut squares

These cookies consist of a chewy coconut layer resting on a crisp chocolate graham cracker base. Cut into squares to serve.

1

Makes 9

8 oz dark chocolate graham crackers

⅓ cup butter or margarine

6 oz canned evaporated milk

1 egg, beaten

1 tsp vanilla extract

5 tsp superfine sugar

⅓ cup self-rising flour, sifted

1½ cups shredded coconut

1¼ oz dark chocolate (optional)

1 Grease a shallow 8-inch square cake pan and line the bottom.

cook's tip

3

2 Crush the crackers in a plastic bag with a rolling pin or process them in a food processor.

3 Melt the butter or margarine in a pan and stir in the crushed crackers until well combined.

4 Press the mixture into the base of the cake pan.

5 Beat together the evaporated milk, egg, vanilla, and sugar until smooth. Stir in the flour and shredded coconut. Pour over the biscuit base and then level the top.

6 Bake in a preheated oven, 375°F, for 30 minutes, or until the coconut topping is firm and just golden.

7 Let cool in the cake pan for about 5 minutes, then cut into squares. Let cool completely in the pan.

5

8 Carefully remove the squares from the pan and place them on a board. Melt the dark chocolate (if using) and then drizzle it over the squares to decorate them. Let the chocolate set before serving.

creamy caramel & oat squares

It is difficult to say "No" to these marvelously rich cookies, which consist of a crunchy base, a creamy caramel filling, and a chocolate top.

1

2

4

Makes 16

generous ⅓ cup soft margarine

4 tbsp light muscovado sugar

1 cup all-purpose flour

⅓ cup rolled oats

CARAMEL FILLING

2 tbsp butter

2 tbsp light muscovado sugar

7 oz canned condensed milk

TOPPING

3½ oz dark chocolate

1 oz white chocolate (optional)

1 Beat together the margarine and muscovado sugar in a bowl until light and fluffy. Beat in the flour and the rolled oats. Use your fingertips to bring the mixture together, if necessary.

2 Press the mixture into the bottom of a shallow 8-inch square cake pan.

3 Bake in a preheated oven, 350°F, for 25 minutes, or until just golden and firm. Let cool in the pan.

4 Place the ingredients for the caramel filling in a pan and heat gently, stirring until the sugar has dissolved and the ingredients combine. Bring slowly to a boil over a very low heat, then boil very gently for 3–4 minutes, stirring constantly until thickened.

5 Pour the caramel filling over the oat base in the pan and let set.

6 Melt the dark chocolate and spread it over the caramel. If using the white chocolate, melt it and pipe lines of white chocolate over the dark chocolate. Using a toothpick or a skewer, feather the white chocolate into the dark chocolate. Let set. Cut into squares to serve.

cook's tip

If desired, you can line the pan with baking parchment so that the whole thing can be lifted out before cutting into pieces.

dairy-free mixed fruit slices

These vegan slices are ideal for packed lunches for children.
They are full of flavor and are made with healthy ingredients.

1

Makes 12

PASTRY

1¼ cups whole-wheat flour

½ cup finely ground mixed nuts

½ cup vegan margarine, cut into small pieces

4 tbsp water

soy milk, to glaze

FILLING

8 oz dried apricots

grated rind of 1 orange

1¼ cups apple juice

1 tsp ground cinnamon

½ cup raisins

2

1 Lightly grease a 9-inch square cake pan. To make the pastry, place the flour and nuts in a mixing bowl and rub in the margarine with your fingers until the mixture resembles bread crumbs. Stir in the water and bring together to form a dough. Wrap and let chill for at least 30 minutes.

2 To make the filling, place the apricots, orange rind, and apple juice in a pan and bring to a boil. Simmer for 30 minutes, or until the apricots are mushy. Cool slightly, then blend to a paste. Stir in the cinnamon and raisins.

3 Divide the pastry in half. Roll out one half and use to line the base of the pan. Spread the apricot paste over the top and brush the edges of the pastry with water. Roll out the rest of the dough to fit over the top of the apricot paste. Press down and seal the edges.

3

4 Prick the top of the pastry with a fork and brush with soy milk. Bake in a preheated oven, 400°F, for 20–25 minutes, or until golden. Let cool slightly before cutting into 12 bars. Serve warm.

cook's tip

These slices will keep in an airtight container for 3-4 days.

raisin and cherry morsels

These delicious creations are more substantial than a crisp cookie.
Serve them fresh from the oven to enjoy them at their best.

2

3

5

3 Stir in the sugar, golden raisins, and chopped candied cherries.

4 Add the beaten egg and the milk to the mixture and mix together to form a soft dough.

5 Spoon 8 mounds of the mixture on to the cookie sheet, spacing them well apart as they will spread while they are cooking.

6 Bake in a preheated oven, 400°F, for 15–20 minutes, or until firm to the touch when pressed with a finger.

7 Remove the morsels from the cookie sheet. Either serve very hot from the oven or transfer to a wire rack and let cool before serving.

Makes 8

1¾ cups all-purpose flour

2 tsp baking powder

¼ cup butter, cut into small pieces

¼ cup brown crystal sugar

½ cup golden raisins

2 tbsp candied cherries, chopped finely

1 egg, beaten

2 tbsp milk

1 Lightly grease a cookie sheet.

2 Sift the flour and baking powder into a mixing bowl. Rub in the butter with your fingers until the mixture resembles bread crumbs.

cook's tip

For convenience, prepare the dry ingredients in advance and stir in the liquid just before cooking.

rosemary & lemon melts

Do not be put off by the idea of herbs being used in these crisp biscuits – try them and you will be pleasantly surprised.

Makes about 25

1¾ oz butter, softened

1¾ oz caster sugar

grated rind of 1 lemon

4 tbsp lemon juice

1 egg, separated

2 tsp finely chopped fresh rosemary

7 oz plain flour, sieved

caster sugar, for sprinkling (optional)

4

5

6

variation

In place of the fresh rosemary, use 1½ teaspoons of dried rosemary, if you prefer.

cook's tip

Store the biscuits in an airtight container for up to 1 week.

1 Lightly grease 2 baking trays.

2 In a large mixing bowl, cream together the butter and sugar until pale and fluffy.

3 Add the lemon rind and juice, then the egg yolk and beat until they are thoroughly combined. Stir in the chopped fresh rosemary.

4 Add the sieved flour, mixing well until a soft dough is formed. Wrap and leave to chill for 30 minutes.

5 On a lightly floured surface, roll out the dough thinly and stamp out about 25 circles with a 6–cm biscuit cutter. Arrange the dough circles on the prepared baking trays.

6 In a bowl, lightly whisk the egg white. Gently brush the egg white over the surface of each biscuit, then sprinkle with a little caster sugar.

7 Bake in a preheated oven, 350°F, for about 15 minutes.

8 Transfer the biscuits to a wire rack and leave to cool before serving.

chocolate chip & golden raisin flapjacks

Turn ordinary flapjacks into something special with the addition of some chocolate chips. Dark chocolate chips are used here, but you could use milk chocolate or white chocolate chips, if preferred.

2

Makes 12

½ cup butter

½ cup superfine sugar

1 tbsp light corn syrup

4 cups rolled oats

½ cup dark chocolate chips

½ cup golden raisins

3

1 Lightly grease a shallow 8-inch square cake pan.

2 Place the butter, superfine sugar, and light corn syrup in a pan and cook over a low heat, stirring until the butter and sugar melt and the mixture is well combined.

3 Remove the pan from the heat and stir in the rolled oats until they are well coated. Add the chocolate chips and the golden raisins and mix well to combine everything.

4 Turn into the prepared pan and press down well.

5 Bake in a preheated oven, 350°F, for 30 minutes. Cool slightly, then mark into fingers. When almost cold, cut into bars or squares and transfer to a wire rack until cold.

3

cook's tip

The flapjacks will keep in an airtight container for up to 1 week, but they are so delicious they are unlikely to last that long!

variation

For a really special flapjack, replace some of the oats with chopped nuts or sunflower seeds and a little extra dried fruit.

chewy cherry flapjacks

Freshly baked, these chewy flapjacks are just the thing for snack-times.

2

Makes 16 squares

1 cup butter

1¼ cups brown crystal sugar

2 tbsp light corn syrup

3½ cups oatmeal

1 cup shredded coconut

¼ cup candied cherries, chopped

3

4

1 Lightly grease a 12 x 9-inch cookie sheet.

2 Heat the butter, brown crystal sugar, and light corn syrup in a large pan, until just melted.

3 Stir in the oats, shredded coconut, and candied cherries and mix well until evenly combined.

4 Spread the mixture on to the cookie sheet and press down with the back of a spatula to make a smooth surface.

5 Bake in a preheated oven, 325°F, for about 30 minutes.

6 Remove from the oven and let cool on the cookie sheet for 10 minutes.

7 Cut the mixture into squares using a sharp knife.

8 Carefully transfer the flapjack squares to a wire rack and let cool completely.

cook's tip

The flapjacks are best stored in an airtight container and eaten within 1 week. They can also be frozen for up to 1 month.

oat & sesame drops

These oaty, fruity cookies are delicious with a cup of coffee!

4

Makes 10

10 tsp butter

½ cup superfine sugar

1 egg, beaten

½ cup all-purpose flour

⅛ tsp salt

½ tsp baking powder

2 cups oatmeal

¼ cup raisins

2 tbsp sesame seeds

5

3 Add the beaten egg gradually and beat until well combined.

4 Sift the flour, salt, and baking powder into the creamed mixture. Mix well.

5 Add the oatmeal, raisins, and sesame seeds and mix together thoroughly.

6 Place spoonfuls of the mixture well apart on the prepared cookie sheets and flatten them slightly with the back of a spoon.

6

variation

Substitute chopped ready-to-eat dried apricots for the raisins, if you prefer.

1 Lightly grease 2 cookie sheets.

2 In a large mixing bowl, cream together the butter and sugar until light and fluffy.

7 Bake in a preheated oven, 350°F, for 15 minutes.

8 Let the cookies cool slightly on the cookie sheets.

9 Transfer the cookies to a wire rack and let them cool completely before serving.

dark chocolate & yogurt muffins

Muffins are always popular and are so simple to make. For young children, mini muffins are marvelous bite-size treats and are perfect for children's parties.

Makes 12

generous ½ cup soft margarine

1 cup superfine sugar

2 large eggs

⅔ cup whole milk unsweetened yogurt

5 tbsp milk

2 cups all-purpose flour

1 tsp baking soda

6 oz dark chocolate chips

2

3

4

3 Sift the flour and baking soda together and add to the mixture. Stir until just blended.

4 Stir in the chocolate chips, then spoon the mixture into the paper cases and bake in a preheated oven, 375°F, for 25 minutes, or until a fine skewer inserted into the center comes out clean. Let cool in the pan for 5 minutes, then turn out on to a wire rack to cool completely.

1 Line 12 muffin pans with paper cases.

2 Place the margarine and sugar in a large mixing bowl and beat with a wooden spoon until light and fluffy. Beat in the eggs, yogurt, and milk until thoroughly combined.

apple biscuits

These biscuits are light and buttery like traditional biscuits, but they have a deliciously rich flavor, which comes from the molasses.

Makes 8

2 cups self-rising flour

1 tbsp superfine sugar

pinch of salt

¼ cup butter, cut into small pieces

1 eating apple, peeled, cored, and chopped

1 egg, beaten

2 tbsp molasses

5 tbsp milk

1 Lightly grease a cookie sheet.

2 Sift the flour, sugar, and salt into a mixing bowl.

3 Rub in the butter with your fingers until the mixture resembles fine bread crumbs.

4 Stir the chopped apple into the mixture until combined.

5 Mix the beaten egg, molasses, and milk together in a pitcher. Add to the dry ingredients to form a soft dough.

6 On a lightly floured counter, roll out the dough to a thickness of ¾ inch and cut out 8 biscuits, using a 2-inch cutter.

7 Arrange the biscuits on the prepared cookie sheet and bake in a preheated oven, 425°F, for 8–10 minutes.

8 Transfer the biscuits to a wire rack and let cool slightly.

9 Serve split in half and spread generously with butter.

4

5

6

cook's tip

These biscuits can be frozen, but are best defrosted and eaten within 1 month.

golden raisin & cherry biscuits

These are an alternative to traditional biscuits, using sweet candied cherries that not only create color but add a distinct flavor.

Makes 8

2 cups self-rising flour

1 tbsp superfine sugar

pinch of salt

¼ cup butter, cut into small pieces

3 tbsp candied cherries, chopped

3 tbsp golden raisins

1 egg, beaten

¼ cup milk

cook's tip

These biscuits will freeze very successfully but they are best defrosted and eaten within 1 month.

3

4

5

1 Lightly grease a cookie sheet.

2 Sift the flour, sugar, and salt into a mixing bowl and rub in the butter with your fingers until the biscuit mixture resembles bread crumbs.

3 Stir in the candied cherries and golden raisins. Add the egg.

4 Reserve 1 tablespoon of the milk for glazing, then add the remainder to the mixture. Mix welll to form a soft dough.

5 On a lightly floured counter, roll out the dough to a thickness of ¾ inch and cut out 8 biscuits, using a 2-inch cutter.

6 Put the biscuits on the cookie sheet and brush with the reserved milk.

7 Bake in a preheated oven, 425°F, for 8–10 minutes, or until the biscuits are golden brown.

8 Let cool on a wire rack, then serve split and buttered.

hazelnut bites

These can be made quickly and easily for an afternoon treat.

The chopped hazelnuts can be replaced by any other nut of your choice.

Makes 16

1¼ cups all-purpose flour

pinch of salt

1 tsp baking powder

⅓ cup butter, cut into small pieces

1 cup soft brown sugar

1 egg, beaten

4 tbsp milk

1 cup hazelnuts, halved

brown crystal sugar, for sprinkling (optional)

variation

For a coffee-time cookie, replace the milk with the same amount of cold strong black coffee—the stronger, the better!

3

4

5

1 Grease a 9-inch square cake pan and line the bottom with baking parchment.

2 Sift the flour, salt, and baking powder into a large mixing bowl.

3 Rub in the butter with your fingers until the mixture resembles fine bread crumbs. Stir in the brown sugar.

4 Add the egg, milk, and nuts to the mixture and stir well until thoroughly combined.

5 Spoon the mixture into the prepared cake pan and level the surface. Sprinkle with brown sugar, if using.

6 Bake in a preheated oven, 350°F, for about 25 minutes, or until the mixture is firm to the touch when pressed with a finger.

7 Let cool for 10 minutes, then loosen the edges with a round-bladed knife and turn out on to a wire rack. Cut into squares.

butter shortbread wedges

These cookies are perfect for afternoon tea or they can be served with ice cream for a delicious dessert.

Makes 8

½ cup butter, softened

8 tsp granulated sugar

8 tsp confectioners' sugar

2 cups all-purpose flour

pinch of salt

2 tsp orange flower water

superfine sugar, for sprinkling (optional)

4

4

cook's tip

For a crunchy addition, sprinkle 2 tablespoons of chopped mixed nuts over the top of the fantails before baking.

4

1 Lightly grease an 8-inch shallow round cake pan.

2 In a large mixing bowl, cream together the butter, the granulated sugar and the confectioners' sugar until light and fluffy.

3 Sift the flour and salt into the creamed mixture. Add the orange flower water and bring everything together to form a soft dough.

4 On a lightly floured surface, roll out the dough to an 8-inch round and place in the pan.

5 Bake in a preheated oven, 300°F, for 30–35 minutes or until the cookie is pale golden and crisp.

6 Sprinkle with superfine sugar, then cut along the marked lines to make the fantails.

7 Leave the shortbread to cool before removing the pieces from the pan. Store in an airtight container.

caraway roundels

The caraway seed is best known for its appearance in old-fashioned seed cake. Here, caraway seeds give these cookies a very distinctive flavor.

Makes about 36

2 cups all-purpose flour

pinch of salt

⅓ cup butter, cut into small pieces

1¼ cups superfine sugar

1 egg, beaten

2 tbsp caraway seeds

brown crystal sugar, for sprinkling (optional)

1 Lightly grease several cookie sheets.

2 Sift the flour and salt into a mixing bowl. Rub in the butter with your fingers until the mixture resembles fine bread crumbs. Stir in the superfine sugar.

3 Reserve 1 tablespoon of the beaten egg for brushing the cookies. Add the rest of the egg to the mixture along with the caraway seeds and bring together to form a soft dough.

variation

Caraway seeds have a nutty, delicate anise flavor. If you don't like this, replace the caraway seeds with the milder-flavored poppy seeds.

2

3

4

4 On a lightly floured counter, roll out the cookie dough thinly and then cut out about 36 rounds with a 2½-inch/6-cm cookie cutter.

5 Transfer the rounds to the prepared cookie sheets, then brush with the reserved egg and sprinkle with a little brown crystal sugar.

6 Bake in a preheated oven, 325°F, for 10–15 minutes, or until lightly golden and crisp.

7 Let the cookies cool on a wire rack and store in an airtight container.

rich chocolate butter shortbread

This buttery chocolate shortbread is the perfect addition to the cookie tin of any chocoholic.

Makes 12

1½ cups all-purpose flour

1 tbsp unsweetened cocoa

4 tbsp superfine sugar

⅔ cup butter, softened

1¾ oz dark chocolate, finely chopped

variation

For round shortbread cookies, roll out the dough on a lightly floured counter to ³/₈ inch thick. Cut out 3-inch circles with a cookie cutter. Transfer to a greased cookie sheet and bake as above. If desired, coat half the cookie in melted chocolate.

1 Lightly grease a cookie sheet.

2 Place all of the ingredients in a large mixing bowl and beat until they form a dough. Knead the dough lightly.

3 Place the dough on the prepared cookie sheet and roll or press out to form an 8-inch circle.

4 Pinch the edges of the dough with your fingertips to form a decorative edge. Prick all over with a fork and mark into 12 wedges, using a sharp knife.

5 Bake in a preheated oven, 325°F, for 40 minutes, or until firm and golden. Let cool slightly before cutting into wedges. Transfer to a wire rack to cool completely.

variation

The dough can be pressed into a floured shortbread mold and turned out on to the cookie sheet before baking.

malted triangles

These are perfect with a bedtime drink, although you can enjoy these tasty cookie wedges at any time of the day.

Makes 16

generous ⅓ cup butter

2 tbsp light corn syrup

2 tbsp malted chocolate drink

8 oz malted milk cookies

2¼ oz milk or dark chocolate,
    broken into pieces

2 tbsp confectioners' sugar

2 tbsp milk

1 Grease a shallow 7-inch round cake pan or tart pan and line the base.

2 Place the butter, light corn syrup, and malted chocolate drink in a small pan and heat gently, stirring all the time until the butter has melted and the mixture is well combined.

2

3

3 Crush the cookies in a plastic bag with a rolling pin, or process them in a food processor until they form crumbs. Stir the crumbs into the chocolate mixture and mix well.

4 Press the mixture into the prepared pan and then chill in the refrigerator until firm.

5 Place the chocolate pieces in a small heatproof bowl with the confectioners' sugar and the milk. Place the bowl over a pan of gently simmering water and stir until the chocolate melts and the mixture is combined.

6

6 Spread the chocolate frosting over the cookie base and let it set in the pan. Using a sharp knife, cut into wedges to serve.

variation

Add chopped pecan nuts to the cookie crumb mixture in step 3, if desired.

rich butter biscuits with chocolate chips

A plain biscuit mixture is transformed into a chocoholic's treat
by the simple addition of chocolate chips.

Makes 9

2 cups self-rising flour, sifted

¼ cup butter

1 tbsp superfine sugar

¼ cup chocolate chips

about ⅔ cup milk

1 Lightly grease a cookie sheet.
Place the flour in a mixing bowl.
Cut the butter into small pieces and rub
it into the flour with your fingertips; do
this until the mixture resembles fine
bread crumbs.

2 Stir in the superfine sugar and
chocolate chips.

3 Mix in enough milk to form a
soft dough.

4 On a lightly floured counter, roll out
the dough to form a rectangle
4 x 6 inches, about 1 inch thick. Cut the
dough into 9 squares.

5 Place the biscuits, spaced well apart
on the prepared cookie sheet.

6 Brush with a little milk and bake in a
preheated oven, 425°F, for 10–12
minutes, or until the biscuits are risen
and golden.

cook's tip

To be at their best, all
biscuits should be freshly
baked and served warm. Split
the warm biscuits and spread
them with a little chocolate
and hazelnut spread or a good
glob of whipped cream.

1

2

4

variation

Use dark, milk, or white
chocolate chips or a mixture
of all three. Use a 2-inch
cookie cutter to cut out round
biscuits, if desired.

frosted orange cookies

These are delicious, melt-in-the-mouth, chocolate cookies with a tangy orange frosting. Children love these cookies, especially if different shapes are used.

Makes about 30

½ cup butter, softened

½ cup superfine sugar

1 egg

1 tbsp milk

2 cups all-purpose flour

¼ cup unsweetened cocoa

FROSTING

1 cup confectioners' sugar, sifted

3 tbsp orange juice

a little dark chocolate, melted

2

3

6

1 Carefully line 2 cookie sheets with baking parchment.

2 Beat together the butter and sugar until light and fluffy. Beat in the egg and milk until well combined. Sift together the flour and unsweetened cocoa and gradually mix together to form a soft dough. Use your fingers to incorporate the last of the flour and to bring the dough together.

3 Roll out the `dough on to a lightly floured counter until ¼ inch thick. Using a 2-inch fluted round cutter, cut out as many cookies as you can. Re-roll the dough trimmings and cut out more cookies.

4 Place the cookies on the prepared cookie sheet and bake in a preheated oven, 350°F, for 10–12 minutes, or until golden.

5 Let the cookies cool on the cookie sheet for a few minutes, then transfer to a wire rack to cool completely.

6 To make the frosting, place the confectioners' sugar in a bowl and stir in enough orange juice to form a thin frosting that will coat the back of a spoon. Spread the frosting over the cookies and let it set. Drizzle with melted chocolate. Let the chocolate set before serving.

chocolate-coated wheat cookies

These are good everyday cookies, and will keep well in an airtight container for at least 1 week. Dip them in white, milk, or dark chocolate.

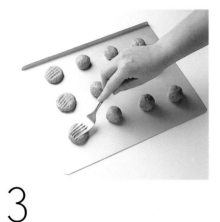

3

Makes about 20

⅓ cup butter

7 tbsp brown crystal sugar

1 egg

1 oz wheatgerm

1 cup whole-wheat self-rising flour

½ cup self-rising flour, sifted

4½ oz chocolate

3

4

cook's tip

These cookies can be frozen very successfully. Freeze them at the end of step 3 for up to 3 months. Defrost and then dip them in melted chocolate.

1 Lightly grease a cookie sheet. Beat the butter and sugar until fluffy. Add the egg and beat well. Stir in the wheatgerm and flours. Bring the mixture together with your hands.

2 Roll rounded teaspoons of the mixture into balls and place on the prepared cookie sheet, allowing room for the cookies to spread during cooking.

3 Flatten the cookies slightly with the prongs of a fork. Bake in a preheated oven, 350°F, for 15–20 minutes, or until golden. Let cool on the sheet for a few minutes before transferring to a wire rack to cool completely.

4 Melt the chocolate, then dip each cookie in the chocolate to cover the bases and come a little way up the sides. Let the excess drip back into the bowl.

5 Place the cookies on a sheet of baking parchment and let them set in a cool place before serving.

orange gingernuts

Nothing compares to the taste of these freshly baked authentic gingernuts, which have a lovely hint of orange.

Makes 30

3 cups self-rising flour

pinch of salt

1 cup superfine sugar

1 tbsp ground ginger

1 tsp baking soda

½ cup butter

¼ cup light corn syrup

1 egg, beaten

1 tsp grated orange rind

3

4

7

1 Lightly grease several cookie sheets.

2 Sift the flour, salt, sugar, ginger, and baking soda into a mixing bowl.

3 Heat the butter and light corn syrup in a pan over a very low heat until the butter has melted.

4 Let the butter mixture cool slightly, then pour it on to the dry ingredients.

5 Add the egg and orange rind and mix thoroughly.

6 Using your hands, carefully shape the dough into 30 even-sized balls.

7 Place the balls well apart on the prepared cookie sheets, then flatten them slightly with your fingers.

8 Bake in a preheated oven, 325°F, for 15–20 minutes, then transfer them to a wire rack to cool.

cook's tip

Store these gingernuts in an airtight container and eat them within 1 week.

variation

If you like your gingernuts crunchy, bake them in the oven for a few minutes longer.

mixed fruit crescents

For a sweet treat, try these cookies which have a lovely citrus tang to them.

Makes about 25

⅓ cup butter, softened

⅓ cup superfine sugar

1 egg, separated

1¾ cups all-purpose flour

grated rind of 1 orange

grated rind of 1 lemon

grated rind of 1 lime

2–3 tbsp orange juice

superfine sugar, for sprinkling (optional)

cook's tip

Store the citrus crescents in an airtight container. Alternatively, they can be frozen for up to 1 month.

3

4

5

1 Lightly grease 2 cookie sheets.

2 In a mixing bowl, cream together the butter and sugar until light and fluffy, then gradually beat in the egg yolk.

3 Sift the flour into the creamed mixture and mix until evenly combined. Add the orange, lemon, and lime rinds to the mixture with enough of the orange juice to make a soft dough.

4 Roll out the dough on a lightly floured counter. Stamp out rounds using a 3-inch cookie cutter. Make crescent shapes by cutting away one fourth of each round. Re-roll the trimmings to make about 25 crescents.

5 Place the crescents on to the prepared cookie sheets. Prick the surface of each crescent with a fork.

6 Lightly whisk the egg white in a small bowl and brush it over the cookies. Dust with extra superfine sugar, if using.

7 Bake in a preheated oven, 400°F, for 12–15 minutes. Let the cookies cool on a wire rack before serving.

dry almond cookies

These dry cookies are delicious served with black coffee after a meal.

Makes 16

1 egg

½ cup superfine sugar

1 tsp vanilla extract

1 cup all-purpose flour

½ tsp baking powder

1 tsp ground cinnamon

1¾ oz dark chocolate,
   coarsely chopped

1¾ oz toasted slivered almonds

1¾ oz pine nuts

1 Grease a large cookie sheet.

2 Whisk the egg, sugar, and vanilla extract in a mixing bowl with an electric mixer until it is thick and pale—ribbons of mixture should trail from the whisk as you lift it.

3 Sift the flour, baking powder, and cinnamon into a separate bowl, then sift into the egg mixture and fold in gently. Stir in the chocolate, almonds, and pine nuts.

2

3

4 Turn out on to a lightly floured counter and shape into a flat log about 9 inches long and ¾ inch wide. Transfer to the prepared cookie sheet.

5 Bake in a preheated oven, 350°F, for 20–25 minutes, or until golden. Remove from the oven and let cool for 5 minutes, or until firm.

6 Transfer the log to a cutting board. Using a serrated bread knife, cut the log on the diagonal into slices about ½ inch thick and arrange them on the cookie sheet. Cook for 10–15 minutes, turning them halfway through the cooking time.

7 Let cool for about 5 minutes, then transfer to a wire rack to cool completely.

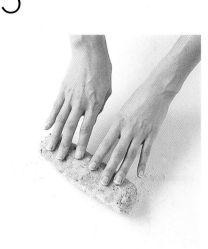

4

cook's tip

Store the cookies in an airtight container or jar and eat within 2 weeks.

sugared lemon cookies

These lemony, melt-in-the-mouth cookies are made extra special by dredging with confectioners' sugar just before serving.

2

Makes about 50

⅛ cup butter, softened

½ cup superfine sugar

grated rind of 1 lemon

1 egg, beaten

4 tbsp lemon juice

3 cups all-purpose flour

1 tsp baking powder

1 tbsp milk

confectioners' sugar, for dredging

4

6

1 Lightly grease several cookie sheets.

2 In a mixing bowl, cream together the butter, superfine sugar, and lemon rind until pale and fluffy.

3 Add the beaten egg and lemon juice a little at a time, beating well after each addition.

4 Sift the flour and baking powder into the creamed mixture and blend together. Add the milk, mixing to form a soft dough.

5 Turn the dough out on to a lightly floured counter and divide into about 50 equal-size pieces.

6 Roll each piece into a sausage shape with your hands and twist in the middle to make an "S" shape.

7 Place on the prepared cookie sheets and bake in a preheated oven, 325°F, for 15–20 minutes. Let cool completely on a wire rack. Dredge with confectioners' sugar to serve.

variation

If you prefer, shape the dough into other shapes—letters of the alphabet or geometric shapes—or just make into round cookies.

spiced rum cookies

These spicy cookies are perfect to serve with
fruit salad or ice cream for a very easy instant dessert.

2

3

5

Makes about 24

¾ cup unsalted butter

1 cup dark muscovado sugar

2 cups all-purpose flour

pinch of salt

½ tsp baking soda

1 tsp ground cinnamon

½ tsp ground coriander

½ tsp ground nutmeg

¼ tsp ground cloves

2 tbsp dark rum

1 Lightly grease 2 cookie sheets.

2 Cream together the butter and sugar and whisk until light and fluffy.

3 Sift the flour, salt, baking soda, cinnamon, coriander, nutmeg, and cloves into the creamed mixture.

4 Pour the dark rum into the creamed mixture and stir well.

5 Using 2 teaspoons, place small mounds of the mixture, on to the cookie sheets, placing them 3 inches apart to allow for spreading during cooking. Flatten each one slightly with the back of a spoon.

6 Bake in a preheated oven, 350°F, for 10–12 minutes, or until golden.

7 Let the cookies cool and become crisp on wire racks before serving.

cook's tip

Use the back of a fork to flatten the cookies slightly before baking.

dark chocolate chip & vanilla cookies

This chocolate chip cookie recipe is sure to be a favorite,
especially since it can be used to make several variations.

variations

For Mixed Chocolate Chip Cookies, use a mixture of dark, milk, and white chocolate chips in the basic mixture.

For Chocolate Chip & Coconut Cookies, add ⅓ cup shredded coconut to the basic mixture.

For Chocolate Chip & Raisin Cookies, add 5 tbsp raisins to the basic mixture.

variations

For Choc & Nut Cookies, add ½ cup chopped hazelnuts to the basic mixture.

For Double Choc Cookies, beat in 1½ oz/40 g melted dark chocolate.

For White Chocolate Chip Cookies, use white chocolate chips instead of the dark chocolate chips.

Makes about 18

1½ cups all-purpose flour

1 tsp baking powder

½ cup soft margarine

½ cup light muscovado sugar

¼ cup superfine sugar

½ tsp vanilla extract

1 egg

⅔ cup dark chocolate chips

1 Lightly grease 2 cookie sheets.

2 Place all of the ingredients in a large mixing bowl and beat until thoroughly combined.

3 Place tablespoonfuls of the mixture on to the cookie sheets, spacing them well apart to allow for spreading during cooking.

4 Bake in a preheated oven, 375°F, for 10–12 minutes, or until the cookies are golden brown.

5 Using a spatula, transfer the cookies to a wire rack to cool completely.

crunchy peanut cookies

These crunchy cookies will be popular with children of all ages, especially since they contain their favorite food—peanut butter.

2

6

cook's tip

For a crunchy bite and sparkling appearance, sprinkle the cookies with brown sugar before baking.

Makes 20

½ cup butter, softened

½ cup chunky peanut butter

1 cup granulated sugar

1 egg, lightly beaten

1¼ cup all-purpose flour

½ tsp baking powder

pinch of salt

½ cup chopped unsalted peanuts

7

1 Lightly grease 2 cookie sheets.

2 In a large mixing bowl, beat together the butter and peanut butter.

3 Gradually add the granulated sugar and beat well.

4 Add the beaten egg to the mixture, a little at a time, until it is thoroughly combined.

5 Sift the flour, baking powder, and salt into the peanut butter mixture.

6 Add the peanuts and bring all of the ingredients together to form a soft dough. Wrap and let chill for about 30 minutes.

7 Form the dough into 20 balls and place them on to the prepared cookie sheets about 2 inches apart to allow for spreading. Flatten them slightly with your hand.

8 Bake in a preheated oven, 375°F, for 15 minutes. Transfer the cookies to a wire rack and let cool.

chocolate & hazelnut tarts

These tasty little tarts will be a big hit with the kids.
Serve them as a dessert or a special snack-time treat.

1

Makes 6

1¾ oz toasted hazelnuts

1¾ cups all-purpose flour

1 tbsp confectioners' sugar

¼ cup soft margarine

FILLING

2 tbsp cornstarch

1 tbsp unsweetened cocoa

1 tbsp superfine sugar

1¼ cups lowfat milk

3 tbsp chocolate and hazelnut spread

2½ tbsp dark chocolate chips

2½ tbsp milk chocolate chips

2½ tbsp white chocolate chips

2

3

1 Finely chop the nuts in a food processor. Add the flour, the 1 tbsp sugar, and the margarine. Process for a few seconds until the mixture resembles bread crumbs. Add 2–3 tbsp water and process to form a soft dough. Cover and chill in the freezer for 10 minutes.

2 Roll out the dough and use it to line six 4-inch loose-bottomed tartlet pans. Prick the bases with a fork and line them with loosely crumpled foil. Bake in a preheated oven, 400°F, for 15 minutes. Remove the foil and bake for an additional 5 minutes, or until the pastry shells are crisp and golden. Remove from the oven and let cool.

3 Mix together the cornstarch, unsweetened cocoa, and sugar with enough milk to make a smooth paste. Stir in the remaining milk. Pour into a pan and cook gently over a low heat, stirring until thickened. Stir in the hazelnut and chocolate spread.

4 Mix together the chocolate chips and reserve one fourth. Stir half of the remaining chips into the custard. Cover with damp waxed paper and let stand until almost cold, then stir in the second half of the chocolate chips. Spoon the mixture into the pastry shells and let cool. Decorate with the reserved chips, scattering them over the top.

Desserts are comforting at any time, but no more so than when served steaming hot. It is hard to think of anything more warming, comforting, and homey than tucking into a rich, steamed Chocolate Dessert or a Chocolate Sponge. The child in us will love the nursery favorites such as Spiced Bread & Butter Dessert. In fact, there are several old favorites that have been given contemporary treatment, bringing them bang up-to-date and putting them firmly on the dessert-lovers' map.

When you are feeling in need of something a little more sophisticated, try the new-style Layered Apple Crêpes, or Pear Tart with Chocolate Sauce, which might be more in keeping. Or try Traditional Italian Zabaglione for a sophisticated, creamy, warm dessert set to get your taste buds in a whirl!

This chapter is packed full of cold delights too, such as Dark & White Chocolate Cheesecake, and a variety of ice-creams, with different tastes and textures to add excitement to any day.

hot & cold
desserts

rum custards with marbled shapes

Wickedly rich little pots, flavored with a hint of dark rum, for pure indulgence!

Serves 6

8 oz dark chocolate

4 eggs, separated

⅓ cup superfine sugar

4 tbsp dark rum

4 tbsp heavy cream

TO DECORATE

a little whipped cream

chocolate shapes (see page 244)

cook's tip

Make sure you use a perfectly clean and grease-free bowl for whisking the egg whites. They will not aerate if any grease is present, because the smallest amount breaks down the bubbles in the whites, preventing them from trapping and holding air.

1

3

4

1 Melt the chocolate and let it cool slightly.

2 Whisk the egg yolks with the superfine sugar in a bowl until very pale and fluffy; this will take about 5 minutes with electric beaters, a little longer with a balloon whisk.

3 Drizzle the chocolate into the mixture and fold in together with the rum and the heavy cream.

4 Whisk the egg whites in a grease-free bowl until standing in soft peaks. Fold the egg whites into the chocolate mixture in 2 batches. Divide the mixture between 6 ramekins, or other individual dishes, and let chill for at least 2 hours.

5 To serve, decorate with a little whipped cream and some small chocolate shapes.

variation

These delicious little pots can be flavored with brandy instead of rum, if preferred.

light & dark chocolate sponges

These individual sponges always look impressive at the end of a meal.

3

Serves 6

½ cup butter, softened

¾ cup soft brown sugar

3 eggs, beaten

pinch of salt

2 tbsp unsweetened cocoa

1 cup self-rising flour

1 oz dark chocolate, finely chopped

2¼ oz white chocolate, finely chopped

SAUCE

½ cup heavy cream

¼ cup soft brown sugar

6 tsp butter

3

1 Lightly grease 6 individual ¾-cup molds.

2 In a bowl, cream together the butter and sugar until pale and fluffy. Beat in the eggs a little at a time, beating well after each addition.

3 Sift the salt, unsweetened cocoa, and flour into the creamed mixture and fold through. Stir the chopped chocolate into the mixture until evenly combined.

4 Divide the mixture between the prepared molds. Lightly grease 6 squares of foil and use them to cover the tops of the molds. Press around the edges to seal.

5 Place the molds in a roasting pan and pour in boiling water to come halfway up the sides of the molds.

6 Bake in a preheated oven, 350°F, for 50 minutes, or until a skewer inserted into the center comes out clean.

5

7 Remove the molds from the roasting pan and set aside while you prepare the sauce.

8 To make the sauce, put the cream, sugar, and butter into a pan and bring to a boil over a gentle heat. Simmer gently until the sugar has dissolved.

9 To serve, run a knife around the edge of each sponge, then turn out on to serving plates. Pour the sauce over the top of the sponges and serve immediately.

apple & apricot crumble

The addition of chocolate in the topping makes this popular dessert even more of a treat. It is a good way of enticing children to eat a fruit dessert.

Serves 4

14 oz canned apricots,
   in unsweetened juice

1 lb cooking apples, peeled
   and thickly sliced

¼ cup all-purpose flour

¼ cup butter

⅔ cup oatmeal

4 tbsp superfine sugar

⅔ cup chocolate chips

variation

Other fruits can be used to make this crumble—fresh pears mixed with fresh or frozen raspberries work well. If you do not use canned fruit, add 4 tablespoons of orange juice to the fresh fruit.

variation

For a double chocolate crumble, replace 1-2 tablespoons of flour with unsweetened cocoa.

1 Lightly grease an ovenproof dish with a small amount of butter or margarine.

2 Drain the apricots, reserving 4 tbsp of the juice. Place the apples and apricots in the prepared ovenproof dish with the reserved apricot juice and toss to mix.

3 Sift the flour into a mixing bowl. Cut the butter into small cubes and rub in with your fingertips until the mixture resembles fine bread crumbs. Stir in the oatmeal, sugar, and chocolate chips.

4 Sprinkle the crumble mixture over the apples and apricots and level the top roughly. Do not press the crumble into the fruit.

5 Bake in a preheated oven, 350°F, for 40–45 minutes, or until the topping is golden. Serve the dessert hot or cold.

cook's tip

You can use dark, milk, or white chocolate chips in this recipe, or use a mixture of all three.

2

3

4

traditional Italian zabaglione

As light as air with a creamy texture, this sophisticated dessert is sure to be a real winner. Since it uses only a little chocolate, choose one with a minimum of 70 per cent cocoa solids for a good flavor.

Serves 2

4 egg yolks

4 tbsp superfine sugar

1¼ oz dark chocolate

1 cup Marsala wine

unsweetened cocoa, to dust

1

3

cook's tip

For an up-to-the minute serving idea, spoon the zabaglione into coffee cups and serve with amaretti cookies to the side.

cook's tip

Make the dessert just before serving because the mixture will separate if left to stand. If it begins to curdle, you may be able to save it if you remove it from the heat immediately and place it in a bowl of cold water to stop the cooking. Whisk furiously until the mixture comes together.

2

1 In a large glass mixing bowl, whisk together the egg yolks and superfine sugar until you have a very pale mixture, using electric beaters.

2 Grate the chocolate finely and fold carefully into the egg mixture. Fold in the wine.

3 Place the mixing bowl over a pan of gently simmering water and set the beaters on the lowest speed or swop to a balloon whisk. Cook gently, whisking continuously until the mixture thickens; take care not to overcook or the mixture will curdle.

4 Spoon the hot mixture into warmed individual glass dishes and dust lightly with unsweeneted cocoa. Serve the zabaglione as soon as possible so that it is warm, light, and fluffy.

creamy chocolate & coffee desserts

These delicious chocolate and coffee-flavored desserts will make a perfect finale to any meal.

Serves 4

8 oz dark chocolate

1 tbsp instant coffee

1¼ cups boiling water

1 envelope gelatin

3 tbsp cold water

1 tsp vanilla extract

1 tbsp coffee-flavored liqueur (optional)

1¼ cups heavy cream

4 chocolate coffee beans

8 amaretti cookies

1 Break the chocolate into small pieces and place in a pan with the coffee. Stir in the boiling water and heat gently, stirring until the chocolate melts.

2 Sprinkle the gelatin over the cold water and let it stand to go spongy, then whisk it into the hot chocolate mixture to dissolve it.

3 Stir in the vanilla extract and coffee-flavored liqueur, if using. Let stand in a cool place until just beginning to thicken; whisk from time to time.

4 Whisk the cream until it is standing in soft peaks, then reserve a little for decorating the desserts and fold the remainder into the chocolate mixture. Spoon into serving dishes and let set.

5 Decorate with the reserved cream and coffee beans and serve with the amaretti cookies.

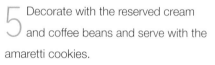

variation

To add a delicious almond flavor to the dessert, replace the coffee-flavored liqueur with almond-flavored liqueur.

cook's tip

If preferred, the desserts can be made in one large serving dish instead.

1

2

4

spiced bread & butter dessert

This is a traditional dessert, which is full of fruit and spices.

It is also the perfect way to use up day-old bread.

2

Serves 6

7 oz white bread, sliced

10 tsp butter, softened

2 tbsp golden raisins

1 oz candied citrus peel

2 ½ cups milk

4 egg yolks

⅓ cup superfine sugar

¼ tsp ground allspice

cook's tip

The dessert can be prepared in advance up to step 7 and then set aside until required.

5

1 Grease a 5⅓-cup ovenproof dish.

2 Remove the crusts from the bread (optional), then spread with butter, and cut into fourths.

3 Arrange half of the bread slices in the prepared ovenproof dish. Sprinkle half of the golden raisins and candied peel over the top of the bread.

4 Place the remaining bread slices over the fruit, and then sprinkle over the reserved fruit.

 To make the custard, bring the milk almost to a boil in a pan. Whisk together the egg yolks and the sugar in a bowl, then pour in the warm milk.

6

6 Strain the warm custard through a strainer. Pour the custard over the bread slices.

7 Let stand for 30 minutes, then sprinkle with the ground allspice.

8 Place the ovenproof dish in a roasting pan half-filled with hot water.

9 Bake in a preheated oven, 400°F, for 40–45 minutes, or until the dessert has just set. Serve warm.

baked plum dessert

This is a favorite dessert which can be adapted to suit all types of fruit if plums are not available.

Serves 6

2 lb plums, pits removed and sliced

⅓ cup superfine sugar

1 tbsp lemon juice

2¼ cups all-purpose flour

⅓ cup granulated sugar

2 tsp baking powder

1 egg, beaten

⅔ cup buttermilk

⅓ cup butter, melted and cooled

heavy cream, to serve

cook's tip

If you cannot find buttermilk, try using sour cream.

3

5

6

1 Lightly grease an 8-cup oven-proof dish.

2 In a large bowl, mix together the plums, superfine sugar, lemon juice, and ¼ cup of the all-purpose flour.

3 Spoon the plums into the bottom of the prepared ovenproof dish.

4 Combine the remaining flour, granulated sugar, and baking powder in a bowl.

5 Add the beaten egg, buttermilk, and cooled melted butter. Mix everything gently together to form a soft dough.

6 Place spoonfuls of the dough on top of the fruit mixture until it is almost covered.

7 Bake in a preheated oven, 375°F, for about 35–40 minutes, or until golden brown and bubbling.

8 Serve the dessert very hot, with heavy cream.

dairy-free mixed fruit crumble

Any fruits in season can be used in this wholesome dessert.
It is suitable for vegans, because it contains no dairy produce.

2

3

Serves 6

6 eating pears, peeled, cored, cut into
   fourths, and sliced
1 tbsp ginger, chopped
1 tbsp dark brown sugar
2 tbsp orange juice

TOPPING
1½ cups all-purpose flour
¼ cup vegan margarine, cut into small pieces
1 oz almonds, slivered
¼ cup oatmeal
1¼ oz dark brown sugar
soy custard, to serve

4

1 Lightly grease a rectangular 4¼-cup ovenproof dish.

2 In a bowl, mix together the pears, ginger, dark brown sugar, and orange juice. Spoon the mixture into the prepared dish.

3 To make the crumble topping, sift the flour into a mixing bowl and rub in the margarine with your fingers until the mixture resembles fine bread crumbs. Stir in the slivered almonds, oatmeal, and dark brown sugar. Mix until well combined.

4 Sprinkle the crumble topping evenly over the pear and ginger mixture in the dish.

5 Bake in a preheated oven, 375°F, for 30 minutes, or until the topping is golden and the fruit tender. Serve with soy custard, if using.

variation

Stir 1 tsp ground allspice into the crumble mixture in step 3 for added flavor, if you prefer.

baked apple & golden raisin dessert

This is a popular family dessert with soft apples on the bottom and a light buttery sponge on top.

2

Serves 6

1 lb cooking apples, peeled, cored, and
    sliced

⅓ cup granulated sugar

1 tbsp lemon juice

⅓ cup golden raisins

⅓ cup butter

⅓ cup superfine sugar

1 egg, beaten

1¼ cups self-rising flour

3 tbsp milk

¼ cup slivered almonds

custard or heavy cream,
    to serve

4

5

cook's tip

To increase the almond flavor
of this pudding, add ¼ cup
ground almonds with the flour
in step 4.

1 Grease a 3½-cup ovenproof dish.

2 Mix the apples with the sugar, lemon
juice, and golden raisins. Spoon the
mixture into the greased dish.

3 In a bowl, cream the butter and
superfine sugar together until pale.
Add the egg, a little at a time.

4 Carefully fold in the self-rising flour
and stir in the milk to give the
mixture a soft, dropping consistency.

5 Spread the mixture evenly over
the apples and sprinkle with the
slivered almonds.

6 Bake in a preheated oven, 350°F, for
40–45 minutes, or until the sponge
is golden brown.

7 Serve the pudding very hot,
accompanied by either custard or
heavy cream.

rich chocolate sponge with fudge sauce

This fabulous steamed sponge, served with a rich chocolate fudge sauce, is perfect for cold winter days—and it can be made in double-quick time in a microwave oven, if you have one.

Serves 6

generous ½ cup soft margarine

1¼ cups self-rising flour

½ cup light corn syrup

3 eggs

¼ cup unsweetened cocoa

CHOCOLATE FUDGE SAUCE

3½ oz dark chocolate

½ cup sweetened condensed milk

4 tbsp heavy cream

2

3

1 Lightly grease a 5-cup mixing bowl.

2 Place the ingredients for the sponge in a mixing bowl and beat until well combined and smooth.

3 Spoon into the prepared bowl and level the top. Cover with a disk of baking parchment and tie a pleated sheet of foil over the bowl. Steam for 1½–2 hours, or until the pudding is cooked and springy to the touch.

4 To make the sauce, break the chocolate into small pieces and place in a small pan with the condensed milk. Heat gently, stirring until the chocolate melts.

5 Remove the pan from the heat and stir in the heavy cream.

6 To serve the sponge, turn it out on to a serving plate and pour over a little of the chocolate fudge sauce. Serve the remaining sauce separately.

cook's tip

To cook the sponge in a microwave oven, cook it, uncovered, on High for 4 minutes, turning the bowl once. Let stand for at least 5 minutes before turning out. While the sponge is standing, make the sauce. Break the chocolate into pieces and place in a microwave-proof bowl with the milk. Cook on High for 1 minute, then stir until the chocolate melts. Stir in the heavy cream and serve.

layered apple hotcakes

If you cannot wait to get your first chocolate "fix" of the day, serve these hotcakes for breakfast. They also make a perfect family dessert.

Serves 4-6

2 cups all-purpose flour

1½ tsp baking powder

4 tbsp superfine sugar

1 egg

1 tbsp butter, melted

1¼ cups milk

1 eating apple

1¾ oz dark chocolate chips

Hot Chocolate Sauce (see page 215) or
    maple syrup, to serve

1

3

4

variation

Milk chocolate chips can be used instead of the dark ones, if preferred.

cook's tip

To keep the cooked hotcakes warm, pile them on top of each other with baking parchment in between to prevent them sticking to each other.

3 Heat a griddle or heavy-based skillet over a medium heat and grease it lightly. For each hotcake, place about 2 tablespoons of the batter on to the griddle or skillet and spread to make a 3-inch round.

4 Cook for a few minutes until you see bubbles appear on the surface of the hotcake. Turn over and cook for 1 minute more. Remove from the skillet and keep warm. Repeat with the remaining batter to make about 12 hotcakes.

5 To serve, stack 2 or 3 hotcakes on an individual serving plate and serve with either the hot chocolate sauce or maple syrup.

1 Sift the flour and baking powder into a mixing bowl. Stir in the superfine sugar. Make a well in the center and add the egg and melted butter. Gradually whisk in the milk to form a smooth batter.

2 Peel and core, then grate the apple and stir it into the batter with the chocolate chips.

eggless tiramisu

This is a traditional chocolate dessert from Italy, although at one time it was known as Zuppa Inglese because it was a favorite with the English society living in Florence in the 1800s.

1

1

cook's tip

Tiramisu can also be served semi-frozen, like ice cream. Freeze the tiramisu for 2 hours and serve immediately because it defrosts very quickly.

Serves 4

10½ oz dark chocolate

14 oz mascarpone cheese

⅔ cup heavy cream, whipped until it just
   holds its shape

1¼ cups black coffee with
   1¼ oz superfine sugar, cooled

6 tbsp dark rum or brandy

36 ladyfingers

about 14 oz unsweetened cocoa,
   to dust

2

variation

Try adding ⅓ cup toasted, chopped hazelnuts to the chocolate cream mixture in step 1, if you prefer.

1 Melt the chocolate in a bowl set over a pan of simmering water, stirring occasionally. Let the chocolate cool slightly, then stir it into the mascarpone and cream.

2 Mix the coffee and rum together in a bowl. Dip the ladyfingers into the mixture briefly so that they absorb the liquid but do not become soggy.

3 Place 3 ladyfingers on each of 3 serving plates.

4 Spoon a layer of the mascarpone and chocolate mixture over the ladyfingers.

5 Place 3 more ladyfingers on top of the mascarpone layer, in a clockwise direction to the ladyfingers on the bottom layer. Spread another layer of mascarpone and chocolate mixture and place 3 more ladyfingers on top, this time in the same direction as the ladyfingers on the bottom layer.

6 Let the tiramisu chill in the refrigerator for at least 1 hour. Dust with a little unsweetened cocoa just before serving.

chocolate gingernut cake

A crumbly ginger chocolate base, topped with velvety smooth chocolate brandy cream, makes this a blissful cake.

Serves 12

BASE

9 oz gingernut cookies

2¾ oz dark chocolate

generous ⅓ cup butter

FILLING

8 oz dark chocolate

9 oz mascarpone cheese

2 eggs, separated

3 tbsp brandy

1¼ cups heavy cream

4 tbsp superfine sugar

TO DECORATE

scant ½ cup heavy cream

chocolate coffee beans

variation

If chocolate coffee beans are unavailable, use chocolate-coated raisins to decorate.

1 Crush the cookies in a bag with a rolling pin or in a food processor. Melt the chocolate and butter together and pour over the cookies. Mix well, then use to line the bottom and sides of a 9-inch loose-bottomed fluted tart pan or springform pan. Let chill while preparing the filling.

2 To make the filling, melt the dark chocolate in a pan, remove from the heat, and beat in the mascarpone, egg yolks, and brandy.

3 Lightly whip the cream until just holding its shape and fold in the chocolate mixture.

4 Whisk the egg whites in a grease-free bowl until standing in soft peaks. Add the superfine sugar a little at a time and whisk until thick and glossy. Fold into the chocolate mixture, in 2 batches, until just mixed.

3

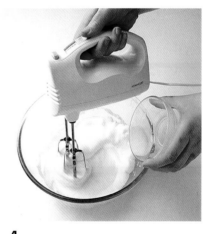

4

5 Spoon the mixture into the prepared base and chill for at least 2 hours. Carefully transfer to a serving plate. To decorate, whip the cream and pipe on to the cheesecake and add the chocolate coffee beans.

banana profiteroles with chocolate sauce

Chocolate profiteroles are a popular choice. In this recipe they are filled with a delicious banana-flavored cream—the perfect combination!

Serves 4-6

CHOUX PASTRY

⅔ cup water

¼ cup butter

½ cup strong all-purpose flour, sifted

2 eggs

CHOCOLATE SAUCE

3½ oz dark chocolate, broken into pieces

2 tbsp water

4 tbsp confectioners' sugar

2 tbsp unsalted butter

FILLING

1¼ cups heavy cream

1 banana

2 tbsp confectioners' sugar

2 tbsp banana-flavored liqueur

1

1

2

1 Lightly grease a cookie sheet and sprinkle with a little water. To make the pastry, place the water in a pan. Cut the butter into small pieces and add to the pan. Heat gently until the butter melts, then bring to a rolling boil. Remove the pan from the heat and add the flour in one go, beating well until the mixture leaves the sides of the pan and forms a ball. Let cool slightly, then gradually beat in the eggs to form a smooth, glossy mixture. Spoon the paste into a large pastry bag fitted with a ½-inch plain tip.

2 Pipe about 18 small balls of the paste on to the cookie sheet, allowing enough room for them to expand during cooking. Bake in a preheated oven, 425°F, for 15–20 minutes, or until crisp and golden. Remove from the oven and make a small slit in each one for steam to escape. Cool on a wire rack.

3 To make the sauce, place all the ingredients in a heatproof bowl, then set over a pan of simmering water, and heat until combined to make a smooth sauce, stirring.

4 To make the filling, whip the cream until standing in soft peaks. Mash the banana with the sugar and liqueur. Fold into the cream. Place in a pastry bag fitted with a ½-inch plain tip and pipe into the profiteroles. Serve with the sauce poured over.

creamy pecan & raisin roulade

The addition of nuts and raisins gives this dessert extra texture, making it similar to that of chocolate brownies.

3

Serves 8

5½ oz dark chocolate,
    broken into pieces

3 tbsp water

¾ cup superfine sugar

5 eggs, separated

2 tbsp raisins, chopped

1 oz pecan nuts, chopped

pinch of salt

1¼ cups heavy cream, whipped lightly

confectioners' sugar, for dusting

4

1 Grease a 12 x 8-inch jelly-roll pan
  and line with baking parchment.
Grease the parchment.

2 Melt the chocolate with the water in
  a small pan over a low heat until the
chocolate has just melted. Let cool.

3 In a bowl, whisk the sugar and egg
  yolks for 2–3 minutes with a hand-
held electric whisk until thick and pale.

4 Fold in the cooled chocolate, raisins,
  and pecan nuts.

5 In a separate bowl, whisk the egg
  whites with the salt. Fold one fourth
of the egg whites into the chocolate
mixture, then fold in the rest of the
whites, working lightly and quickly.

6 Transfer the mixture to the prepared
  pan and bake in a preheated oven,
350°F, for 25 minutes, or until risen and
just firm to the touch. Let
cool before covering with a sheet of non-
stick baking parchment and a clean,
damp dish towel. Let stand until
completely cold.

5

7 Turn out the roulade on to another
  piece of baking parchment dusted
with confectioner's sugar and then
remove the lining paper.

8 Spread the cream over the roulade.
  Starting from a short end, roll the
sponge away from you using the paper
to guide you. Trim the ends of the
roulade to make a neat finish and
transfer to a serving plate. Let chill in the
refrigerator until ready to serve. Dust with
a little confectioners' sugar before
serving, if wished.

creamy chocolate sponge

In this recipe, the mixture separates out during cooking to produce a cream sponge topping and a delicious chocolate sauce on the bottom.

Serves 4

1¼ cups milk

2¾ oz dark chocolate

½ tsp vanilla extract

7 tbsp superfine sugar

generous ⅓ cup butter

1¼ cups self-rising flour

2 tbsp unsweetened cocoa

confectioners' sugar, to dust

FOR THE SAUCE

3 tbsp unsweetened cocoa

4 tbsp light muscovado sugar

1¼ cups boiling water

variation

For a mocha sauce, add 1 tbsp instant coffee to the unsweetened cocoa and sugar in step 4, before mixing to a paste with the boiling water.

2

3

4

1 Lightly grease an 3¾-cup oven-proof dish.

2 Place the milk in a small pan. Break the chocolate into pieces and add to the milk. Heat gently, stirring until the chocolate melts. Let cool slightly. Stir in the vanilla extract.

3 Beat together the superfine sugar and butter in a bowl until light and fluffy. Sift together the flour and unsweetened cocoa. Add to the bowl with the chocolate milk and beat until smooth, using an electric whisk if you have one. Pour the mixture into the prepared dish.

4 To make the sauce, mix together the unsweetened cocoa and sugar. Add a little boiling water and mix to a smooth paste, then stir in the remaining water. Pour the sauce over the sponge, but do not mix it in.

5 Place the dish on to a cookie sheet and bake in a preheated oven, 350°F, for 40 minutes, or until springy to the touch. Let stand for about 5 minutes, then dust with a little confectioners' sugar just before serving.

banana crêpes with hot chocolate sauce

Crêpes are given the chocolate treatment here to make a rich and fabulous, dessert to round off a dinner party. Prepare this recipe ahead of time for easy trouble-free entertaining.

2

Serves 4

3 large bananas

6 tbsp orange juice

grated rind of 1 orange

2 tbsp orange- or banana-flavored liqueur

HOT CHOCOLATE SAUCE

1 tbsp unsweetened cocoa

2 tsp cornstarch

3 tbsp milk

1½ oz dark chocolate

1 tbsp butter

½ cup light corn syrup

¼ tsp vanilla extract

CRÊPES

1 cup all-purpose flour

1 tbsp unsweetened cocoa

1 egg

1 tsp sunflower oil

1¼ cups milk

oil, for cooking

3

1 Peel and slice the bananas and arrange them in a dish with the orange juice and rind and the liqueur. Set aside.

2 For the sauce, mix the unsweetened cocoa and cornstarch in a bowl, then stir in the milk. Break the dark chocolate into pieces and place in a pan with the butter and light corn syrup. Heat gently, stirring until well blended. Add the cocoa mixture and bring to a boil over a gentle heat, stirring. Simmer for 1 minute, then remove from the heat and stir in the vanilla extract.

3

3 To make the crêpes, sift the flour and cocoa into a mixing bowl and make a well in the center. Add the egg and oil. Gradually whisk in the milk to form a smooth batter. Heat a little oil in a heavy-based skillet and pour off any excess. Pour in a little batter and tilt the skillet to coat the bottom. Cook over a medium heat until the underside is browned. Flip over and cook the other side. Slide the crêpe out of the skillet and keep warm. Repeat until all the batter has been used.

4 To serve, reheat the chocolate sauce for 1–2 minutes. Fill the crêpes with the bananas and fold in half or into triangles. Pour over a little chocolate sauce and serve.

rich pecan ring

Although this pecan ring can be served cold as a cake, it is
absolutely delicious served hot as a dessert.

2

Serves 6

FUDGE SAUCE

3 tbsp butter

3 tbsp light brown sugar

4 tbsp light corn syrup

2 tbsp milk

1 tbsp unsweetened cocoa

1½ oz dark chocolate

1¼ oz pecan nuts, finely chopped

CAKE

generous ¼ cup soft margarine

7 tbsp light brown sugar

1 cup self-rising flour

2 eggs

2 tbsp milk

1 tbsp light corn syrup

3

4

1 Lightly grease an 8-inch ring pan.

2 To make the fudge sauce, place the
butter, sugar, syrup, milk, and
unsweetened cocoa in a small pan and
heat gently. Keep stirring until combined.

3 Break the chocolate into pieces.
Add to the mixture and stir until
melted. Stir in the chopped pecan nuts.
Pour into the bottom of the pan and
let cool.

4 To make the cake, place all of the
ingredients in a mixing bowl and
beat until smooth. Spoon the cake
mixture over the chocolate fudge sauce.

5 Bake in a preheated oven, 350°F, for
35 minutes, or until the cake is
springy to the touch.

6 Let cool in the pan for 5 minutes,
then turn out on to a serving dish
and serve.

cook's tip

To make in a microwave oven,
place the butter, sugar,
syrup, milk, and unsweetened
cocoa for the sauce in a
microwave-proof bowl. Cook on
High for 2 minutes, stirring
twice. Stir in the chocolate
until melted, then add the
nuts. Pour into a 5 cup
microwave-proof ring mold.
Make the cake and cook on High
for 3-4 minutes until just dry
on top; stand for 5 minutes.

crumbly chocolate, apple & cinnamon pie

This easy-to-make chocolate pastry encases a delicious apple filling studded with chocolate chips. This recipe is guaranteed to become a family favorite.

Serves 6

CHOCOLATE PASTRY

4 tbsp unsweetened cocoa

1¾ cups all-purpose flour

¾ cup softened butter

4 tbsp superfine sugar

2 egg yolks

few drops of vanilla extract

cold water, to mix

FILLING

1 lb 10 oz cooking apples

2 tbsp butter

½ tsp ground cinnamon

¾ cup dark chocolate chips

a little egg white, beaten

½ tsp superfine sugar

whipped cream or vanilla ice cream, to serve

3

4

4

1 To make the pastry, sift the unsweetened cocoa and flour into a mixing bowl and rub in the butter until the mixture resembles fine bread crumbs. Stir in the sugar. Add the egg yolks, vanilla extract, and enough water to mix to a dough.

2 Roll out the dough on a lightly floured counter and use to line a deep 8-inch tart pan or cake pan. Chill for 30 minutes. Roll out any trimmings and cut out some pastry leaves to decorate the top of the pie.

3 Peel and core, then thickly slice the apples. Place half of the apple slices in a pan with the butter and cinnamon and cook over a gently heat, until the apples soften.

4 Stir in the uncooked apple slices, let cool slightly, and stir in the chocolate chips. Prick the base of the pie shell and pile the apple mixture into it. Arrange the pastry leaves on top. Brush the leaves with a little egg white and sprinkle with superfine sugar.

5 Bake in a preheated oven, 350°F, for 35 minutes, or until the pastry is crisp. Serve warm or cold, with whipped cream or vanilla ice cream.

raspberry & cream shortbread

For this lovely summery dessert, two crisp rounds of shortbread are sandwiched together with fresh raspberries and lightly whipped cream.

Serves 8

1½ cups self-rising flour

½ cup butter, cut into cubes

½ cup superfine sugar

1 egg yolk

1 tbsp rose water

2½ cups whipping cream, whipped lightly

8 oz raspberries, plus a few for decoration

TO DECORATE

confectioners' sugar

mint leaves

cook's tip

The shortcake can be made a few days in advance and stored in an airtight container until required.

3

4

1 Lightly grease 2 cookie sheets.

2 To make the shortbread, sift the flour into a bowl.

3 Rub the butter into the flour with your fingers until the mixture resembles bread crumbs.

5

4 Stir the sugar, egg yolk, and rose water into the mixture and bring together with your fingers to form a soft dough. Divide the dough in half.

5 Roll each piece of dough to an 8-inch round and lift each one on to a prepared cookie sheet. Crimp the edges of the dough.

6 Bake in a preheated oven, 375°F, for 15 minutes, or until lightly golden. Transfer the shortbread to a wire rack and let cool.

7 Mix the cream with the raspberries and spoon on top of one of the shortbread circles. Top with the other shortbread circle, then dust with a little confectioners' sugar, and decorate with the extra raspberries and mint leaves.

mixed fruit pavlova

This delicious dessert originated in Australia. Serve it with
sharp fruits to balance the sweetness of the meringue.

Serves 6

3 egg whites

pinch of salt

¾ cup superfine sugar

1¼ cups heavy cream, lightly whipped

fresh fruit of your choice (raspberries,

   strawberries, peaches, passion fruit,

   ground cherries)

1 Carefully line a cookie sheet with a sheet of baking parchment.

2 Whisk the egg whites with the salt in a bowl until they form soft peaks.

3 Whisk in the superfine sugar a little at a time, whisking well after each addition until all of the sugar has been incorporated.

4 Spoon three-fourths of the meringue on to the cookie sheet, forming a circle 8 inches in diameter.

5 Place spoonfuls of the remaining meringue all around the edge of the circle so that they join up to make a nest shape.

6 Bake in a preheated oven, 275°F, for 1¼ hours.

7 Turn the heat off, but let the pavlova stand in the oven until it is completely cold.

8 To serve, place the pavlova on a serving dish. Spread with the lightly whipped cream, then arrange the fresh fruit on top.

variation

If you are worried about making the round shape, draw a circle on the baking parchment, turn the paper over, and spoon the meringue inside the shape.

cook's tip

It is a good idea to make the pavlova in the evening and leave it in the turned-off oven overnight.

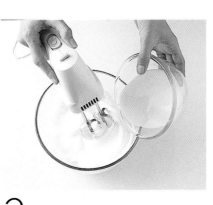

2

3

5

sweet blackberry dessert

A delicious dessert to make when blackberries are in abundance!
If blackberries are unavailable, use other fruits such as currants or gooseberries.

Serves 4

1 lb blackberries

¼ cup superfine sugar

1 egg

¼ cup soft brown sugar

¼ cup butter, melted

8 tbsp milk

4½ oz self-rising flour

1 Lightly grease a large 3½-cup ovenproof dish.

2 In a large mixing bowl, gently mix together the blackberries and superfine sugar until well combined.

3 Transfer the blackberry and sugar mixture to the ovenproof dish.

4 Beat the egg and soft brown sugar in a separate mixing bowl. Stir in the melted butter and milk.

5 Sift the flour into the egg and butter mixture and fold together lightly to form a smooth batter.

6 Carefully spread the batter over the blackberry and sugar mixture in the ovenproof dish.

7 Bake the dessert in a preheated oven, 350°F, for about 25–30 minutes, or until the topping is firm and golden.

8 Sprinkle the dessert with a little sugar and serve hot.

3

5

6

variation

You can add 2 tablespoons of unsweetened cocoa to the batter in step 5, if you prefer a chocolate flavor.

sweet pear & ginger pastries

These tarts are made with ready-made puff pastry, which is available from most supermarkets. The final result is rich and buttery.

2

Serves 6

9 oz fresh ready-made puff pastry

1 oz soft brown sugar

1 oz butter (plus extra for brushing)

1 tbsp candied ginger, finely chopped

3 pears, peeled, halved, and cored

cream, to serve

5

6

cook's tip

If you prefer, serve these pastries with vanilla ice cream for a delicious dessert.

1 On a lightly floured counter, roll out the pastry. Cut out six 4-inch circles.

2 Place the circles on to a large cookie sheet and let chill for 30 minutes.

3 Cream together the brown sugar and butter in a small bowl, then stir in the chopped candied ginger.

4 Prick the pastry circles with a fork and spread a little of the ginger mixture on to each one.

5 Slice the pear halves lengthwise— but keeping them intact at the tip. Fan out the slices slightly.

6 Place a fanned-out pear half on top of each pastry circle. Make small flutes around the edge of the pastry circles and brush each pear half with melted butter.

7 Bake in a preheated oven, 400°F, for 15–20 minutes, or until the pastry is well risen and golden. Serve warm with a little cream.

sweet mincemeat pastry

This pastry makes a good Thanksgiving dessert. Its
filling and flavor provide a great alternative to mincemeat.

4

Serves 4

1 lb fresh ready-made puff pastry

14½ oz mincemeat

3½ oz grapes, seeded and halved

1 egg, for glazing

brown sugar, for sprinkling

cook's tip

For an enhanced festive flavor, stir 2 tbsp sherry into the mincemeat.

5

1 Lightly grease a cookie sheet.

2 On a lightly floured counter, roll out the pastry and cut it into 2 oblongs.

3 Place one pastry oblong on to the prepared cookie sheet and brush the edges with water.

4 Combine the mincemeat and grapes in a mixing bowl. Spread the mixture over the pastry oblong on the baking sheet, leaving a 1-inch border.

5 Fold the second pastry oblong in half lengthwise, and carefully cut a series of parallel lines across the folded edge, leaving a 1-inch border.

6 Open out the pastry oblong and lay it over the mincemeat. Seal down the edges of the and press together well.

7 Flute and crimp the edges of the pastry. Brush with the beaten egg and sprinkle with brown sugar.

6

8 Bake in a preheated oven, 425°F, for 15 minutes. Lower the heat to 350°F and cook for an additional 30 minutes, or until the pastry is well risen and golden brown. Let cool on a wire rack before serving.

dairy-free pineapple cake

This upside-down cake shows how a classic favorite can be adapted for vegans by making the cake with vegan margarine and oil instead of butter and eggs.

Serves 6

15 oz canned unsweetened pineapple pieces, drained and juice reserved

4 tsp cornstarch

3 tbsp soft brown sugar

10 tsp vegan margarine, cut into small pieces

½ cup water

rind of 1 lemon

SPONGE

¼ cup sunflower oil

⅓ cup soft brown sugar

⅔ cup water

1¼ cups all-purpose flour

2 tsp baking powder

1 tsp ground cinnamon

2

3

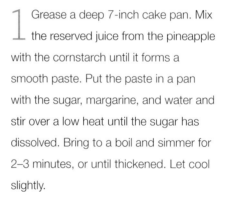

3

variation

You can add 1 oz golden raisins to the pineapple pieces, if you prefer.

1 Grease a deep 7-inch cake pan. Mix the reserved juice from the pineapple with the cornstarch until it forms a smooth paste. Put the paste in a pan with the sugar, margarine, and water and stir over a low heat until the sugar has dissolved. Bring to a boil and simmer for 2–3 minutes, or until thickened. Let cool slightly.

2 To make the sponge, place the oil, sugar, and water in a pan. Heat gently until the sugar has dissolved; do not let it boil. Remove from the heat and let cool. Sift the flour, baking powder, and ground cinnamon into a mixing bowl. Pour over the cooled sugar syrup and beat well to form a batter.

3 Place the pineapple pieces and lemon rind on the bottom of the pan and pour over 4 tablespoons of the pineapple syrup. Spoon the sponge batter on top.

4 Bake in a preheated oven, 350°F, for 35–40 minutes, or until set and a fine metal skewer inserted into the center comes out clean. Invert on to a plate and let stand for 5 minutes, then remove the pan. Serve with the remaining syrup.

caramelized cream tartlets

Serve these tarts with fresh fruit, if desired.

2

Makes 6

PASTRY

1¼ cups all-purpose flour

5 tsp superfine sugar

½ cup butter, cut into small pieces

1 tbsp water

FILLING

4 egg yolks

1¾ oz superfine sugar

1¼ cups heavy cream

1 tsp vanilla extract

brown crystal sugar, for sprinkling

4

1 To make the pastry, place the flour and sugar in a bowl and rub in the butter with your fingers. Add the water and work the mixture together until a soft pastry has formed. Wrap and let chill for 30 minutes.

2 On a lightly floured counter, roll out the dough to line six 4-inch tart pans. Prick the bottom of the pastry with a fork and let chill for 20 minutes.

3 Line the pastry shells with foil and baking beans and bake in a preheated oven, 375°F, for 15 minutes. Remove the foil and beans and cook for 10 minutes, or until crisp and golden. Let cool.

4 Meanwhile, make the filling. In a bowl, beat the egg yolks and sugar until pale. Heat the cream and vanilla extract in a pan until just below boiling point, then pour it onto the egg mixture, whisking constantly.

5 Return the mixture to a clean pan and bring to just below a boil, stirring, until thick. Do not let it boil or it will curdle.

6 Let the mixture cool slightly, then pour it into the tart pans. Let cool and then chill overnight.

7 Sprinkle the tarts with the sugar. Place under a preheated hot broiler for a few minutes. Let cool, then chill for 2 hours before serving.

7

orange & marmalade meringue

This is a slightly different version of the old favorite, made with the addition of orange rind and marmalade to give a delicious orange flavor.

Serves 8

2½ cups milk

6 tsp butter

1¼ cups superfine sugar

finely grated rind of 1 orange

4 eggs, separated

¼ cup fresh bread crumbs

pinch of salt

6 tbsp orange marmalade

1 Grease a 6-cup ovenproof dish.

2 To make the custard, heat the milk in a pan with the butter, ¼ cup of the superfine sugar, and the grated orange rind until just warm.

3 Whisk the egg yolks in a bowl. Gradually pour the warm milk over the eggs, stirring.

4 Stir the bread crumbs into the pan, then transfer the mixture to the prepared dish and let stand for 15 minutes.

5 Bake in a preheated oven, 350°F, for 20–25 minutes, or until the custard has just set. Remove the custard from the oven, but do not turn the oven off.

6 To make the meringue, whisk the egg whites with a pinch of salt until they stand in soft peaks. Whisk in the remaining sugar, a little at a time.

7 Spread the orange marmalade over the cooked custard. Top with the meringue, spreading it right to the edges of the dish.

8 Return the dessert to the oven and bake for an additional 20 minutes, or until the meringue is crisp and golden.

3

6

7

cook's tip

If you prefer a crisper meringue, bake the dessert in the oven for an extra 5 minutes.

chocolate sponge dessert

This chocolate dessert, consisting of a rich chocolate mousselike filling enclosed in ladyfingers, is a variation of a popular classic.

5 Whisk the egg whites until standing in stiff peaks, then gradually add the superfine sugar, whisking until stiff and glossy. Carefully fold the egg whites into the chocolate mixture in 2 batches, taking care not to knock out all of the air. Pour into the center of the mold. Trim the lady's fingers so that they are level with the chocolate mixture. Let chill for at least 5 hours.

6 To decorate, whisk the cream, sugar, and vanilla extract until standing in soft peaks. Turn out the dessert on to a serving dish. Pipe cream rosettes around the bottom and then decorate with chocolate curls and leaves.

2

Serves 8

about 22 ladyfingers

4 tbsp orange-flavored liqueur

9 oz dark chocolate

½ pint heavy cream

4 eggs

¼ cup superfine sugar

TO DECORATE

⅔ cup whipping cream

2 tbsp superfine sugar

½ tsp vanilla extract

large dark chocolate curls (see page 50),

   chocolate leaves (see page 100), or

   chocolate shapes (see page 244)

3

1 Line the bottom of a Charlotte mold or a deep 7-inch round cake pan with a piece of baking parchment.

2 Place the ladyfingers on a tray and sprinkle with half of the orange-flavored liqueur. Use to line the sides of the mold or pan, trimming if necessary to make a tight fit.

3 Break the chocolate into small pieces. Place in a bowl and melt over a pan of hot water. Remove from the heat and stir in the heavy cream.

4 Separate the eggs and place the whites in a large grease-free bowl. Beat the egg yolks thoroughly into the chocolate mixture.

5

creamy chocolate meringue

Crumbly cracker base and a rich, creamy, chocolate filling topped with fluffy meringue—what could be more indulgent than this fabulous dessert?

1

Serves 6

8 oz dark chocolate graham crackers

4 tbsp butter

FILLING

3 egg yolks

4 tbsp superfine sugar

4 tbsp cornstarch

2½ cups milk

3½ oz dark chocolate, melted

MERINGUE

2 egg whites

7 tbsp superfine sugar

¼ tsp vanilla extract

4

1 Place the graham crackers in a plastic bag and crush with a rolling pin. Pour into a mixing bowl. Melt the butter and stir it into the cracker crumbs until well mixed. Press the cracker mixture firmly into the base and up the sides of a 9-inch tart pan or dish.

2 To make the filling, beat the egg yolks, superfine sugar, and cornstarch in a large bowl until they form a smooth paste, adding a little of the milk if necessary. Heat the milk until almost boiling, then slowly pour it on to the egg mixture, whisking well.

3 Return the mixture to the pan and cook gently, whisking constantly until it thickens. Remove from the heat. Whisk in the melted chocolate, then pour it on to the graham cracker base.

4 To make the meringue, whisk the egg whites in a large mixing bowl until standing in soft peaks. Gradually whisk in about two-thirds of the sugar until the mixture is stiff and glossy. Fold in the remaining sugar and vanilla extract.

5 Spread the meringue over the filling, swirling the surface with the back of a spoon to give it an attractive finish. Bake in a preheated oven, 375°F, for 30 minutes, or until the meringue is golden. Serve hot or just warm.

classic mississippi mud pie

This is an all-time favorite with chocoholics—the "mud" refers
to the gooey, rich chocolate layer of the cake.

Serves 8-10

2 cups all-purpose flour

¼ cup unsweetened cocoa

½ cup butter

5 tsp superfine sugar

about 2 tbsp cold water

FILLING

¾ cup butter

12 oz dark brown sugar

4 eggs, lightly beaten

4 tbsp unsweetened cocoa, sifted

5½ oz dark chocolate

1¼ cups light cream

1 tsp chocolate extract

TO DECORATE

1¼ cups heavy cream, whipped

thick bar of dark chocolate

4

5

6

1   To make the pie dough, sift the flour
and unsweetened cocoa into a
mixing bowl. Rub in the butter until the
mixture resembles fine breadcrumbs. Stir
in the sugar and enough cold water to
mix to a soft dough. Chill for 15 minutes.

2   Roll out the dough on a lightly
floured counter and use to line a
deep 9-inch loose-bottomed tart pan
or ceramic tart dish. Line with foil or
baking parchment and baking beans.
Bake blind in a preheated oven, 375°F,
for 15 minutes. Remove the beans and
foil or paper and cook for an additional
10 minutes, or until crisp.

3   To make the filling, beat the butter
and sugar in a bowl and gradually
beat in the eggs with the unsweetened
cocoa. Melt the chocolate and beat it
into the mixture with the light cream and
the chocolate extract.

4   Pour the mixture into the cooked
pastry case. Bake at 325°F for 45
minutes, or until the filling is set.

5   Let cool completely, then transfer
the pie to a serving plate,
if preferred. Cover with the whipped
cream and let chill.

6   To make small chocolate curls, use
a potato peeler to remove curls from
the bar of chocolate. Decorate the pie
and let chill.

rich chocolate custards

Chocoholics will adore these creamy desserts consisting of a rich baked chocolate custard with the delicious flavor of hazelnuts.

Serves 6

2 eggs

2 egg yolks

1 tbsp superfine sugar

1 tsp cornstarch

2½ cups milk

3 oz dark chocolate

4 tbsp chocolate and hazelnut spread

TO DECORATE

grated chocolate or large chocolate curls

(see page 50)

cook's tip

This dish is traditionally made in little pots called pots de crème, which are individual ovenproof dishes with a lid. Ramekins are fine. The dessert can also be made in one large dish; cook for about 1 hour, or until set.

2

3

1 Beat together the eggs, egg yolks, superfine sugar, and cornstarch until well combined. Heat the milk until it is almost boiling.

2 Gradually pour the milk on to the eggs, whisking as you do so. Melt the chocolate and hazelnut spread in a bowl set over a pan of gently simmering water, then whisk the melted chocolate mixture into the eggs.

3

3 Pour into 6 small ovenproof dishes and cover the dishes with foil. Place them in a roasting pan. Fill the pan with boiling water to come halfway up the sides of the dishes.

4 Bake in a preheated oven, 325°F, for 35–40 minutes, or until the custard is just set. Remove from the pan and cool, then chill until required. Serve decorated with grated chocolate or chocolate curls.

cook's tip

The foil lid prevents a skin forming on the surface of the custards.

chocolate creams with marbled shapes

These rich, creamy desserts are completely irresistible.
Serve them with crisp dessert cookies.

Serves 4

2 cups heavy cream

⅓ cup superfine sugar

1 vanilla pod

¾ cup crème fraîche

2 tsp gelatin

3 tbsp water

1¾ oz dark chocolate

MARBLED CHOCOLATE SHAPES

a little melted white chocolate

a little melted dark chocolate

1

6

1 Place the cream and sugar in a pan. Cut the vanilla pod into 2 pieces and add to the cream. Heat gently, stirring until the sugar has dissolved, then bring to a boil. Reduce the heat and let simmer for 2–3 minutes.

2 Remove the pan from the heat and take out the vanilla pod. Stir in the crème fraîche.

3 Sprinkle the gelatin over the water in a small heatproof bowl and let it go spongy, then place over a pan of hot water and stir until dissolved. Stir into the cream mixture. Pour half of this mixture into another mixing bowl.

6

4 Melt the dark chocolate and stir it into one half of the cream mixture. Pour the chocolate mixture into 4 individual glass serving dishes and chill for 15–20 minutes, or until just set. While it is chilling, keep the vanilla mixture at room temperature.

5 Spoon the vanilla mixture on top of the chocolate mixture and chill until the vanilla is set.

6 Meanwhile, make the shapes for the decoration. Spoon the melted white chocolate into a paper pastry bag and snip off the tip. Spread some melted dark chocolate on a piece of baking parchment. While still wet, pipe a fine line of white chocolate in a scribble over the top. Use the tip of a toothpick to marble the white chocolate into the dark. When firm but not too hard, cut into shapes with a small shaped cutter or a sharp knife. Chill the shapes until firm, then use to decorate the desserts.

mint chocolate desserts

The classic combination of chocolate and mint flavors makes
a delicious dessert for special occasions.

Serves 6

1¼ cups heavy cream

⅔ cup creamy fromage blanc

2 tbsp confectioners' sugar

1 tbsp crème de menthe

6 oz dark chocolate

chocolate, to decorate

2

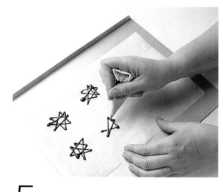

5

cook's tip

Pipe the patterns freehand
or draw patterns on to baking
parchment first, then turn
the parchment over and pipe
the chocolate, following the
drawn outline.

5

1 Place the cream in a large mixing
bowl and then whisk until standing in
soft peaks.

2 Fold in the fromage blanc and
confectioners' sugar, then place
about one-third of the mixture in a
smaller bowl. Stir the crème de menthe
into the smaller bowl. Melt the dark
chocolate and then stir it into the
remaining mixture.

3 Place alternate spoonfuls of the
2 mixtures into serving glasses, then
swirl the mixture together to give a
decorative effect. Let chill until required.

4 To make the piped chocolate
decorations, melt a small amount
of chocolate and place it in a paper
pastry bag.

5 Place a sheet of baking parchment
on a board and pipe squiggles,
stars, or flower shapes with the melted
chocolate. Alternatively, to make curved
decorations, pipe decorations on to a
long strip of baking parchment, then
carefully place the strip over a rolling pin,
securing with sticky tape. Let the
chocolate set, then carefully remove from
the baking parchment.

6 Decorate each dessert with piped
chocolate decorations and serve.
Alternatively, the desserts can be
decorated and then chilled, if preferred.

chocolate butter cream trifle

Try all the delightful flavors of a Black Forest Layer Cake
in this new guise—the results are stunning.

Serves 6-8

6 thin slices chocolate butter cream cake

1 lb12 oz canned black cherries

2 tbsp kirsch

1 tbsp cornstarch

2 tbsp superfine sugar

1¼ cups milk

3 egg yolks

1 egg

2¾ oz dark chocolate

1¼ cups heavy cream, lightly whipped

TO DECORATE

dark chocolate, melted

maraschino cherries (optional)

1 Place the slices of chocolate cake in the bottom of a glass serving bowl.

2 Drain the black cherries, reserving 6 tbsp of the juice. Place the cherries and the reserved juice on top of the cake. Sprinkle with the kirsch.

3 In a bowl, mix the cornstarch and superfine sugar. Stir in enough of the milk to mix to a smooth paste. Beat in the egg yolks and the whole egg.

2

4 Heat the remaining milk in a small pan until almost boiling, then gradually pour it on to the egg mixture, whisking well until it is combined.

5 Place the bowl over a pan of hot water and cook over a low heat until the custard thickens, stirring. Add the chocolate and stir until melted.

6 Pour the chocolate custard over the cherries and cool. When cold, spread the cream over the custard, swirling with the back of a spoon. Chill before decorating.

7 To make chocolate caraque, spread the melted dark chocolate on a marble or acrylic board. As it begins to set, pull a knife through the chocolate at a 45° angle, working quickly. Remove each caraque as you make it and chill firmly before using.

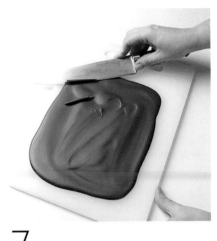

6

7

cranberry & almond tart

This tart is ideal to make at Thanksgiving, when fresh cranberries are in abundance. If desired, brush the warm tart with 2 tbsp melted apricot jelly.

2

4

5

1 To make the pastry, place the flour and sugar in a bowl and rub in the butter with your fingers. Add the water and work the mixture together until a soft pastry has formed. Wrap and let chill for 30 minutes.

2 On a lightly floured counter, roll out the dough and line a 9½-inch loose-bottomed tart pan. Prick the pastry with a fork and let chill for 30 minutes.

3 Line the pie shell with foil and baking beans and bake in a preheated oven, 375°F, for 15 minutes. Remove the foil and baking beans and cook for an additional 10 minutes.

4 To make the filling, cream together the butter and sugar until light and fluffy. Beat in the egg and egg yolks, then stir in the flour, almonds, and cream.

5 Place the apricot halves and cranberries on the bottom of the pie shell and spoon the filling over the top.

6 Bake in the oven for about 1 hour, or until the topping is just set. Let cool slightly, then serve warm or cold.

Serves 8-10

PASTRY

¼ cups all-purpose flour

½ cup superfine sugar

½ cup butter, cut into small pieces

1 tbsp water

FILLING

1 cup unsalted butter

1 cup superfine sugar

1 egg

2 egg yolks

6 tbsp all-purpose flour, sifted

1½ cups ground almonds

4 tbsp heavy cream

14½ oz canned apricot halves, drained

4½ oz fresh cranberries

sweet mincemeat tart

The fresh apple brings out the flavor of the sweet rich mincemeat and makes it a beautifully moist filling for pies and tarts.

Serves 8

PASTRY

1¼ cups all-purpose flour

5 tsp superfine sugar

½ cup butter, cut into small pieces

1 tbsp water

FILLING

14½ oz mincemeat

3 eating apples, cored and grated

1 tbsp lemon juice

6 tsp light corn syrup

9 tsp butter

variation

Add 2 tbsp sherry to spice up the mincemeat, if you wish.

4

5

6

1 To make the pastry, place the flour and superfine sugar in a large mixing bowl and rub in the butter thoroughly with your fingertips.

2 Add the water and work the mixture together until a soft pastry has formed. Wrap and let chill in the refrigerator for 30 minutes.

3 On a lightly floured counter, roll out the dough and line a 9½-inch loose-bottomed tart pan. Prick the dough with a fork and let chill for 30 minutes.

4 Line the pie shell with foil and baking beans. Bake the shell in a preheated oven, 375°F, for 15 minutes. Remove the foil and beans and cook for 15 minutes.

5 Combine the mincemeat with the apples and lemon juice and spoon into the baked pie shell.

6 Melt the syrup and butter together and then pour it evenly over the mincemeat mixture.

7 Return the tart to the oven and bake for about 20 minutes, or until firm. Serve warm.

date & walnut tart

The chopped apples and dates and the soft brown sugar in the filling make this a sweet tart with a savory twist!

2

Serves 8

1 ½ cups self-rising flour

1 tsp baking powder

pinch of salt

¼ cup soft brown sugar

3½ oz pitted dates, chopped

1lb eating apples, cored and chopped

¼ cup walnuts, chopped

¼ cup sunflower oil

2 eggs

6 oz Leicester or colby cheese, grated

3

5

cook's tip

This is a deliciously moist tart. Any leftovers should be stored in the refrigerator and heated to serve.

1 Grease a 9½-inch loose-bottomed tart pan and line it smoothly with baking parchment.

2 Sift the flour, baking powder, and salt into a bowl. Stir in the brown sugar and the chopped dates, apples, and walnuts. Mix them together until thoroughly combined.

3 Beat together the oil and eggs and add them to the dry ingredients. Stir until they are well combined.

4 Spoon half of the mixture into the pan and level the surface with the back of a spoon.

5 Sprinkle with the cheese, then spoon over the remaining cake mix, spreading it to the edges of the pan.

6 Bake in a preheated oven, 350°F, for 45–50 minutes, or until golden and firm to the touch.

7 Let cool slightly in the tin. Serve the tart warm.

buttery lemon tart

No-one will be able to resist this tart with its buttery pastry
and a sharp, melt-in-the-mouth lemon filling.

1

Serves 8

PASTRY

1¼ cups all-purpose flour

5 tsp superfine sugar

½ cup butter, cut into small pieces

1 tbsp water

FILLING

⅔ cup heavy cream

½ cup superfine sugar

4 eggs

grated rind of 3 lemons

12 tbsp lemon juice

confectioners' sugar, for dusting

2

1 To make the pastry, place the flour and sugar in a bowl and rub in the butter using your fingers. Add the water and mix until a soft pastry has formed. Wrap and let chill for 30 minutes.

2 On a lightly floured counter, roll out the dough and line a 9½-inch loose-bottomed tart pan. Prick the pastry with a fork and let chill for 30 minutes.

3 Line the pie shell with foil and baking beans and bake in a preheated oven, 375°F, for 15 minutes. Remove the foil and baking beans and cook for an additional 15 minutes.

4 To make the filling, whisk the cream, sugar, eggs, lemon rind, and juice together. Place the pie shell, still in its pan, on a cookie sheet and then pour in the filling.

4

5 Bake in the oven for about 20 minutes, or until just set. Let cool, then lightly dust with confectioners' sugar before serving.

cook's tip

To avoid any spillage, pour half of the filling into the pie shell, then place in the oven and pour in the remaining filling.

sweet almond tart

This is a variation on the classic pecan pie recipe—here nuts and chocolate are encased in a thick syrup filling.

Serves 8

PASTRY

1¼ cups all-purpose flour

5 tsp superfine sugar

½ cup butter, cut into small pieces

1 tbsp water

FILLING

½ cup light corn syrup

1¾ oz butter

⅓ cup soft brown sugar

3 eggs, lightly beaten

½ cup whole blanched almonds,
　　coarsely chopped

3½ oz white chocolate,
　　coarsely chopped

cream, to serve (optional)

---

variation

You can use a mixture of white and dark chocolate for this tart, if preferred.

2

1 To make the pastry, place the flour and sugar in a mixing bowl and rub in the butter with your fingers. Add the water and work the mixture together until a soft pastry has formed. Wrap and let chill for 30 minutes.

2 On a lightly floured counter, roll out the dough and line a 9½-inch loose-bottomed tart pan. Prick the pastry with a fork and let chill for 30 minutes. Line the pie shell with foil and baking beans and bake in a preheated oven, 375°F, for 15 minutes. Remove the foil and baking beans and cook for an additional 15 minutes.

3 To make the filling, gently melt the syrup, butter, and sugar together in a pan. Remove from the heat and let cool slightly. Stir in the beaten eggs, almonds, and chocolate.

3

4 Pour the chocolate and nut filling into the prepared pie shell and cook in the oven for 30–35 minutes, or until just set. Let cool before removing the tart from the pan. Serve with cream, if desired.

pear tart with chocolate sauce

This attractive dessert consists of a tart filled with pears cooked in a chocolate, almond-flavored sponge. It is delicious served hot or cold.

Serves 6

¾ cup all-purpose flour

¼ cup ground almonds

¼ cup block margarine

about 3 tbsp water

FILLING

14 oz canned pear halves,
   in unsweetened juice

4 tbsp butter

4 tbsp superfine sugar

2 eggs, beaten

1 cup ground almonds

2 tbsp unsweetened cocoa

few drops of almond extract

confectioners' sugar, to dust

CHOCOLATE SAUCE

4 tbsp superfine sugar

3 tbsp light corn syrup

⅓ cup water

6 oz dark chocolate, broken into pieces

2 tbsp butter

2

3

1 Lightly grease an 8-inch tart pan. Sift the flour into a mixing bowl and stir in the almonds. Rub in the margarine with your fingertips until the mixture resembles bread crumbs. Add enough water to mix to a soft dough. Cover, chill in the freezer for 10 minutes, then roll out and use to line the pan. Prick the bottom and chill.

2 To make the filling, drain the pears well. Beat the butter and sugar until light and fluffy. Beat in the eggs. Fold in the almonds, unsweetened cocoa and almond extract. Spread the chocolate mixture in the pie shell and arrange the pears on top, pressing down lightly. Bake in the center of a preheated oven, 400°F, for 30 minutes, or until the filling has risen. Cool slightly and transfer to a serving dish, if wished. Dust with sugar.

3

3 To make the sauce, place the sugar, syrup, and water in a pan and heat gently, stirring until the sugar dissolves. Boil gently for 1 minute. Remove from the heat, add the chocolate and butter, and stir until melted. Serve with the pear tart.

cheese & orange tart

This tart has a sweet filling made with creamed cottage cheese and it is topped with pine nuts for a decorative finish.

1

Serves 8

PASTRY

¼ cups all-purpose flour

5 tsp superfine sugar

½ cup butter, cut into small pieces

1 tbsp water

FILLING

12 oz creamed cottage cheese

4 tbsp heavy cream

3 eggs

½ cup superfine sugar

grated rind of 1 orange

3½ oz pine nuts

2

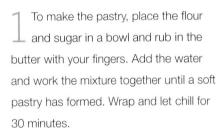

1 To make the pastry, place the flour and sugar in a bowl and rub in the butter with your fingers. Add the water and work the mixture together until a soft pastry has formed. Wrap and let chill for 30 minutes.

2 On a lightly floured counter, roll out the dough and line a 9½-inch loose-bottomed tart pan. Prick the pie dough with a fork and let chill for 30 minutes.

3 Line the pie shell with foil and baking beans and bake in a preheated oven, 375°F, for 15 minutes. Remove the foil and beans and cook the pie shell for an additional 15 minutes.

4

4 To make the filling, beat together the creamed cottage cheese, cream, eggs, sugar, orange rind, and half of the pine nuts. Pour the filling into the pie shell and sprinkle over the remaining pine nuts.

5 Bake in the oven at 325°F for 35 minutes, or until just set. Let cool before serving.

variation

Replace the pine nuts with slivered almonds, if you prefer.

creamy orange tart with bread crumbs

This is a variation of the classic lemon tart—in this recipe
fresh bread crumbs are used to create a thicker texture.

4

4

5

Serves 6-8

PASTRY

1¼ cups all-purpose flour

5 tsp superfine sugar

½ cup butter, cut into small pieces

1 tbsp water

FILLING

grated rind of 2 oranges

9 tbsp orange juice

1 cup fresh white bread crumbs

2 tbsp lemon juice

⅔ cup light cream

¼ cup butter

¼ cup superfine sugar

2 eggs, separated

pinch of salt

1 To make the pastry, place the flour
and sugar in a bowl and rub in the
butter with your fingers. Add the cold
water and work the mixture together until
a soft pastry has formed. Wrap and let
chill for 30 minutes.

2 Roll out the dough and line a
9½-inch loose-bottomed tart pan.
Prick the dough with a fork and let chill
for 30 minutes.

3 Line the pie shell with foil and baking
beans and bake in a preheated
oven, 375°F, for 15 minutes. Remove the
foil and beans and cook for an additional
15 minutes.

4 To make the filling, mix the orange
rind and juice and the bread crumbs
in a bowl. Stir in the lemon juice and light
cream. Melt the butter and sugar in a
pan over a low heat. Remove the pan
from the heat, then add the 2 egg yolks,
the salt, and the bread crumb mixture,
and stir.

5 In a mixing bowl, whisk the egg
whites with a pinch of salt until they
form soft peaks. Fold them into the egg
yolk mixture.

6 Pour the filling mixture into the pie
shell. Bake in a preheated oven,
325°F, for about 45 minutes,
or until just set. Let cool slightly and
serve warm.

chocolate & banana cheesecake

The exotic combination of banana and coconut goes well with chocolate, as illustrated in this lovely cheesecake. You can use shredded coconut, but fresh coconut will give a better flavor.

Serves 10

8 oz chocolate chip cookies

4 tbsp butter

12 oz medium-fat soft cheese

⅓ cup superfine sugar

1¾ oz fresh coconut, grated

2 tbsp coconut-flavored liqueur

2 ripe bananas

4½ oz dark chocolate

1 envelope gelatin

3 tbsp water

⅔ cup heavy cream

TO DECORATE

1 banana

lemon juice

a little melted chocolate

cook's tip

To crack the coconut, pierce 2 of the "eyes" and drain off the liquid. Tap hard around the center with a hammer until it cracks; lever apart.

1

2

4

1 Place the cookies in a plastic bag and crush with a rolling pin. Pour into a mixing bowl. Melt the butter and stir into the cookie crumbs until well coated. Firmly press the cookie mixture into the base and up the sides of an 8-inch springform pan.

2 Beat together the soft cheese and sugar until well combined, then beat in the grated coconut and coconut-flavored liqueur. Mash the 2 bananas and beat them in. Melt the dark chocolate and beat in until well combined.

3 Sprinkle the gelatin over the water in a heatproof bowl and let it go spongy. Place over a pan of hot water and stir until dissolved. Stir into the chocolate mixture. Whisk the cream until just holding its shape and stir into the chocolate mixture. Spoon over the cookie base and chill until set.

4 To serve, carefully transfer to a serving plate. Slice the banana and toss in the lemon juice, then arrange around the edge of the cheesecake. Drizzle with melted chocolate and let set.

dark & white chocolate cheesecake

A dark and white chocolate cheesecake filling is marbled together here to give an attractive finish to this rich and decadent dessert.

3

Serves 10-12

BOTTOM

8 oz toasted oat cereal

½ cup toasted hazelnuts, chopped

4 tbsp butter

1 oz dark chocolate

FILLING

12 oz full-fat soft cheese

7 tbsp superfine sugar

¾ cup thick yogurt

1¼ cups heavy cream

1 envelope gelatin

3 tbsp water

6 oz dark chocolate, melted

6 oz white chocolate, melted

4

6

1 Place the toasted oat cereal in a plastic bag and crush with a rolling pin. Pour the crushed cereal into a mixing bowl and stir in the hazelnuts.

2 Melt the butter and chocolate together over low heat and then stir into the cereal mixture, stirring until thoroughly coated.

3 Using the bottom of a glass, press the mixture into the bottom and up the sides of an 8-inch springform pan.

cook's tip

For a lighter texture, fold in 2 egg whites whipped to soft peaks before folding in the cream in step 4.

4 Beat together the cheese and sugar with a wooden spoon until smooth. Beat in the yogurt. Whip the cream until just holding its shape and fold into the mixture. Sprinkle the gelatin over the water in a heatproof bowl and let it go spongy. Place over a pan of hot water and stir until dissolved. Stir into the mixture.

5 Divide the mixture in half and beat the dark chocolate into one half and the white chocolate into the other half.

6 Place alternate spoonfuls of mixture on top of the cereal bottom. Swirl the filling together with the tip of a knife to give a marbled effect. Level the top with a scraper or a spatula. Let chill until set before serving.

bean curd & ground cherry cheesecake

This cheesecake takes a little time to prepare and cook, but it is well worth the effort. It is quite rich and is good served or decorated with a little fresh fruit, such as sliced strawberries.

Serves 12

¾ cup all-purpose flour

¾ cup ground almonds

¾ cup brown crystal sugar

10 tbsp vegetarian margarine

1½ lb firm bean curd

¾ cup vegetable oil

½ cup orange juice

¾ cup brandy

6 tbsp unsweetened cocoa, plus extra
   to decorate

2 tsp almond extract

confectioners' sugar and ground cherries,
   to decorate

cook's tip

Ground cherries make an attractive decoration for many desserts. Peel open the papery husks to expose the bright orange fruits.

1

1 Put the flour, ground almonds, and 1 tablespoon of the sugar in a bowl, and mix well. Rub the margarine into the mixture to form a dough.

2 Lightly grease and line the base of a 9-inch springform pan. Press the dough into the base of the pan to cover, pushing the dough right up to the edge of the pan.

3 Coarsely chop the bean curd and put in a food processor with all of the remaining ingredients and blend until smooth and creamy. Pour over the base in the pan and cook in a preheated oven, 325°F, for 1–1¼ hours, or until set.

2

3

4 Let cool in the pan for 5 minutes, then remove, and chill in the refrigerator. Dust with confectioners' sugar and unsweetened cocoa. Decorate and serve.

creamy champagne cups

A wonderful champagne-flavored mouse is served in chocolate sponge cups to create this elegant dessert. Any dry sparkling wine made by the traditional method used for champagne can be used.

1

Serves 4

SPONGE

4 eggs

7 tbsp superfine sugar

⅔ cup self-rising flour

2 tbsp unsweetened cocoa

2 tbsp butter, melted

MOUSSE

1 envelope gelatin

3 tbsp water

1¼ cups champagne

1¼ cups heavy cream

2 egg whites

⅓ cup superfine sugar

TO DECORATE

2 oz dark chocolate-flavored cake covering, melted

fresh strawberries

1 Line a 15 x 10-inch jelly-roll pan with greased baking parchment. Place the eggs and sugar in a bowl and whisk with electric beaters until the mixture is very thick and the whisk leaves a trail when lifted. If using a balloon whisk, stand the bowl over a pan of hot water while whisking. Sift the flour and cocoa together and fold into the egg mixture. Fold in the butter. Pour into the pan and bake in a preheated oven, 400°F, for 8 minutes, or until springy to the touch. Cool for 5 minutes, then turn out on to a wire rack until cold. Line four 4-inch baking rings with baking parchment. Line the sides with 1 inch strips of cake and the bottoms with circles.

2 To make the mousse, sprinkle the gelatin over the water and let it go spongy. Place the bowl over a pan of hot water; stir until dissolved. Stir in the champagne.

3 Whip the cream until just holding its shape. Fold in the champagne mixture. Let stand in a cool place until on the point of setting, stirring. Whisk the egg whites until standing in soft peaks, then add the sugar, and whisk until glossy. Fold into the setting mixture. Spoon into the sponge cases, letting the mixture go above the sponge. Chill for 2 hours. Pipe the cake covering in squiggles on a piece of parchment; let them set. Decorate the mousses.

3

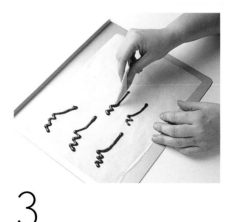

3

light & dark chocolate mousse

Three layers of fabulous rich mousse give this elegant dessert extra chocolate appeal. It is a little fiddly to prepare, but well worth the extra effort.

3

Serves 8

3 eggs

1 tsp cornstarch

4 tbsp superfine sugar

1¼ cups milk

1 envelope gelatin

3 tbsp water

1¼ cups heavy cream

2¾ oz dark chocolate

2¾ oz white chocolate

2¾ oz milk chocolate

chocolate caraque, to decorate
  (see page 249)

1 Line a 1-lb loaf pan with baking parchment. Separate the eggs, putting each egg white in a separate bowl. Place the egg yolks, cornstarch, and sugar in a large mixing bowl and whisk until well combined. Place the milk in a pan and heat gently, stirring until almost boiling. Pour the milk on to the egg yolks, whisking continually.

2 Set the bowl over a pan of gently simmering water and cook, stirring, until the mixture thickens enough to thinly coat the back of a wooden spoon.

3 Sprinkle the gelatin over the water in a small heatproof bowl and let it go spongy. Place over a pan of hot water and stir until dissolved. Stir into the hot mixture. Let cool.

4 Whip the cream until just holding its shape. Fold into the egg custard, then divide the mixture into three. Melt the 3 types of chocolate separately. Fold the dark chocolate into one egg custard portion. Whisk one egg white until standing in soft peaks and fold into the dark chocolate custard until combined. Pour into the prepared pan and level the top. Chill in the coldest part of the refrigerator until just set. Let the remaining mixtures stand at room temperature.

4

5

5 Fold the white chocolate into another portion of the egg custard. Whisk another egg white and fold in. Pour on top of the dark chocolate layer and chill quickly. Repeat with the remaining milk chocolate and egg white. Chill until set. To serve, carefully turn out on to a serving dish and decorate with chocolate caraque.

brandied chocolate & orange mousse

This is a light and fluffy, but fruity-tasting mousse, which
is delicious with a fresh fruit sauce. It is suitable for vegetarians.

Serves 8

3½ oz dark chocolate, melted

1¼ cups unsweetened yogurt

⅔ cup Quark/low-fat curd cheese

4 tbsp superfine sugar

1 tbsp orange juice

1 tbsp brandy

1½ tsp gelozone (vegetarian gelatin),
    or 1 envelope gelatin

9 tbsp cold water

2 large egg whites

coarsely grated dark and white chocolate
    and orange zest, to decorate

cook's tip

For a quick fruit sauce,
blend a can of mandarin
segments in unsweetened juice
in a food processor and press
through a strainer. Stir in
1 tbsp clear honey and serve
with the mousse.

3

4

5

1 Put the melted chocolate,
unsweetened yogurt, Quark,
superfine sugar, orange juice, and
brandy in a food processor, and blend
for 30 seconds. Transfer the mixture to
a large bowl.

2 Sprinkle the gelozone over the water
and stir until dissolved.

3 In a small pan, bring the gelozone
and water to a boil for 2 minutes.
Let cool slightly, then stir into the
chocolate mixture.

4 Whisk the egg whites until stiff peaks
form and fold into the chocolate
mixture using a metal spoon.

5 Line a 3½-cup loaf pan with plastic
wrap. Spoon the mousse into the
pan. Chill for 2 hours in the refrigerator
until set. Turn the mousse out on to a
plate, decorate, and serve.

frozen white chocolate mousse

This iced dessert is somewhere between a chocolate mousse and an ice cream.
Serve it with a chocolate sauce, or a fruit coulis and fresh fruit.

1

2

Serves 8-10

2 tbsp granulated sugar

5 tbsp water

10½ oz white chocolate

3 eggs, separated

1¼ cups heavy cream

1 Line a 1-lb loaf pan with foil or plastic wrap, pressing out as many creases as you can.

2 Place the granulated sugar and water in a heavy-bottomed pan and heat gently, stirring until the sugar has dissolved. Bring to a boil and boil for 1–2 minutes until syrupy, then remove the pan from the heat.

3

3 Break the white chocolate into small pieces and stir it into the syrup, continuing to stir until the chocolate has melted and combined with the syrup. Let cool slightly.

4 Beat the egg yolks thoroughly into the chocolate mixture. Let cool completely.

5 Lightly whip the cream until just holding its shape and fold it into the chocolate mixture.

6 Whisk the egg whites in a grease-free bowl until they are standing in soft peaks. Fold into the chocolate mixture. Pour into the prepared loaf pan and freeze overnight.

7 To serve, remove from the freezer about 10–15 minutes before serving. Turn out of the pan and then cut into slices to serve.

spiced chocolate & almond loaf

This rich chocolate dessert loaf is very simple to make and can also be served as a snack-time treat.

1

2

cook's tip

When baking or cooking with fat, butter has the finest flavor. If possible, it is best to use unsalted butter as an ingredient in puddings and desserts, unless stated otherwise in the recipe. "Low-fat" spreads are not suitable for cooking.

Makes 16 slices

2¾ oz almonds

5½ oz dark chocolate

6 tbsp butter, unsalted

7¼ oz canned condensed milk

2 tsp cinnamon

2¾ oz amaretti crackers, broken

1¾ oz dried no-need-to-soak apricots, coarsely chopped

1 Line a 1½-lb loaf pan with a sheet of kitchen foil.

2 Using a sharp knife, coarsely chop the almonds.

3 Place the chocolate, butter, milk, and cinnamon in a heavy-bottomed pan. Heat gently over a low heat for 3–4 minutes, stirring with a wooden spoon, until the chocolate has melted. Beat the mixture well.

4 Stir the almonds, crackers, and apricots into the chocolate mixture in the pan, stirring with a wooden spoon, until well mixed.

5 Pour the mixture into the prepared pan and let chill in the refrigerator for about 1 hour, or until set.

6 Cut the rich chocolate loaf into slices to serve.

cook's tip

To melt chocolate, first break it into manageable pieces. The smaller the pieces, the quicker it will melt.

3

frozen chocolate ring

Hidden in a ring of chocolate cake lies the secret to this freezer cake—a chocolate and mint ice cream. You can use orange or coffee ice cream if you prefer.

Serves 8-10

4 eggs

¾ cup superfine sugar

¾ cup self-rising flour

3 tbsp unsweetened cocoa

2¼ cups chocolate and mint ice cream

Hot Chocolate Sauce

(see page 215)

1 Lightly grease a 9-inch ring pan. Place the eggs and sugar in a large mixing bowl. Using an electric whisk if you have one, whisk the mixture until it is very thick and the whisk leaves a trail. If you are using a balloon whisk, stand the bowl over a pan of hot water while whisking.

2 Sift the flour and cocoa together and fold them into the egg mixture. Pour into the prepared pan and bake in a preheated oven, 350°F, for 30 minutes, or until springy to the touch. Let cool in the pan before turning out on to a wire rack to cool completely.

3 Rinse the cake pan and line with a strip of plastic wrap, overhanging slightly. Cut the top off the cake about ½ inch thick and set aside.

4 Return the cake to the pan. Using a spoon, scoop out the center of the cake, leaving a shell about ½ inch thick.

3

4

5 Remove the ice cream from the freezer and let stand for a few minutes, then beat with a wooden spoon until softened a little. Fill the center of the cake with the ice cream, leveling the top. Replace the top of the cake.

6 Cover with the overhanging plastic wrap and freeze for at least 2 hours.

7 To serve, turn the cake out on to a serving dish and drizzle over some of the chocolate sauce in an attractive pattern, if you wish. Cut the cake into slices and serve the remaining sauce separately.

5

chocolate ice-cream & meringue pie

This is a cool dessert that leaves the cook completely unflustered. Light meringue tops chocolate ice cream for this divine dessert—you can assemble it in advance and pop into the freezer until required.

Serves 6

2 eggs

4 tbsp superfine sugar

generous ¼ cup all-purpose flour

2 tbsp unsweetened cocoa

3 egg whites

⅔ cup superfine sugar

4½ cups good-quality chocolate ice cream

cook's tip

This dessert is delicious served with a blackcurrant coulis. Cook a few blackcurrants in a little orange juice until soft, puree and push through a strainer. Sweeten to taste with a little confectioners' sugar.

4

5

6

1 Grease a 7-inch round cake pan and line the bottom with baking parchment.

2 Whisk the egg and the 4 tbsp sugar in a mixing bowl until very thick and pale. Sift together the flour and unsweetened cocoa and carefully fold in.

3 Pour into the prepared pan and bake in a preheated oven, 425°F, for 7 minutes, or until springy to the touch. Transfer to a wire rack to cool completely.

4 Whisk the egg whites in a grease-free bowl until they are standing in soft peaks. Gradually add the ⅔ cup sugar, whisking until you have a thick, glossy meringue.

5 Place the sponge on a cookie sheet and pile the ice cream on to the center in a heaped dome.

6 Pipe or spread the meringue over the ice cream, making sure the ice cream is completely enclosed. (At this point the pie can be frozen, if wished.)

7 Return it to the oven for 5 minutes, or until the meringue is just golden. Serve immediately.

chocolate ice cream in trellis cups

A richly flavored chocolate ice cream that is delicious served on its own or with a chocolate sauce. For a special dessert, serve in attractive trellis cups.

3

7

Serves 6-8

ICE CREAM

1 egg

3 egg yolks

6 tbsp superfine sugar

1¼ cups whole milk

9 oz dark chocolate

1¼ cups heavy cream

TRELLIS CUPS

3½ oz dark chocolate

1 Beat together the egg, egg yolks, and superfine sugar in a mixing bowl until well combined. Heat the milk until almost boiling.

2 Gradually pour the hot milk on to the eggs, whisking as you do so. Place the bowl over a pan of gently simmering water and cook, stirring, until the mixture thickens sufficiently to thinly coat the back of a wooden spoon.

3 Break the dark chocolate into small pieces and add to the hot custard. Stir until the chocolate has melted. Cover with a sheet of dampened baking parchment and let cool.

4 Whip the cream until just holding its shape, then fold into the cooled chocolate custard. Transfer to a freezer container and freeze for 1–2 hours, or until the mixture is frozen 1 inch from the sides.

5 Scrape the ice cream into a chilled bowl and beat again until smooth. Re-freeze until firm.

6 To make the trellis cups, invert a muffin pan and cover 6 alternate mounds with plastic wrap. Melt the chocolate, place it in a paper pastry bag, and snip off the end.

7 Pipe a circle around the base of the mound, then pipe chocolate back and forth over it to form a trellis; carefully pipe a double thickness. Pipe around the base again. Chill until set, then lift from the pan and remove the plastic wrap. Serve the ice cream in the trellis cups.

7

ice cream in a chocolate cup

This white-chocolate ice cream is served in a chocolate cup.

If desired, top with a chocolate sauce for a true chocolate-addict's treat.

Serves 6

ICE CREAM

1 egg

1 egg yolk

3 tbsp superfine sugar

5¼ oz white chocolate

1¼ cups milk

⅔ cup heavy cream

COOKIE CUPS

1 egg white

4 tbsp superfine sugar

2 tbsp all-purpose flour, sifted

2 tbsp unsweetened cocoa, sifted

2 tbsp butter, melted

2

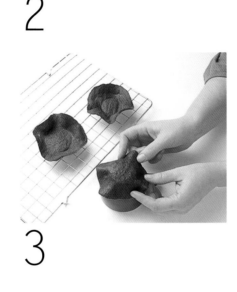

3

1 Place baking parchment on 2 cookie sheets. To make the ice cream, beat together the egg, egg yolks, and sugar. Break the chocolate into pieces, place in a bowl with 3 tablespoons of milk, and melt over a pan of hot water. Heat the milk until almost boiling and pour on to the eggs, whisking. Place over a pan of simmering water and cook, stirring, until the mixture thickens enough to coat the back of a wooden spoon. Whisk in the chocolate. Cover with dampened baking parchment and let cool.

3

2 Whip the cream until just holding its shape and fold into the custard. Transfer to a freezer container and freeze the mixture for 1–2 hours, or until frozen 1 inch from the sides. Scrape into a bowl and beat again until smooth. Re-freeze until firm.

3 To make the cups, beat the egg white and sugar together. Beat in the flour and cocoa, then the butter. Place 1 tablespoon of mixture on one sheet; spread out to a 5-inch circle. Bake in a preheated oven, 400°F, for 4–5 minutes. Remove and mold over an upturned cup. Let set, then cool on a wire rack. Repeat to make 6 cups. Serve the ice cream in the cups.

Freshly baked bread has never been easier to make, especially with the rising yeasts available nowadays. In this chapter, $\frac{1}{4}$-oz envelopes of rapid-rise dried yeast have been used, because it is easy to obtain, simple to use, and gives good results. If you want to use fresh yeast, replace one envelope of

quick-rising yeast with 1 cake of compressed fresh yeast (each tiny square cake is equal to 0.06 oz). Blend the fresh yeast into the warm liquid and add a pinch of sugar. Let stand for 5-10 minutes, until foaming, then add to the flour and continue as usual. Always choose a white or brown bread flour for the bread recipes that use yeast, because it contains a high proportion of gluten, the protein which gives the dough its elasticity. Always knead the dough thoroughly—this can be done in an electric mixer with the dough hook attachment for about 5-8 minutes. However, kneading by hand is most enjoyable and gives the cook the pleasure of taking out any tension and stress on the dough! This chapter also includes a selection of savories to enjoy, including tasty pies, pastries, and tarts to create a whole medley of delicious dishes that can be used as part of an entrée.

bread
& savory bakes

sage & garlic ring

This freshly made bread is an ideal accompaniment to salads. It is also suitable for vegans.

Serves 4-6

2¼ cups brown bread flour

1 envelope rapid-rise dried yeast

3 tbsp chopped fresh sage

2 tsp sea salt

3 garlic cloves, finely chopped

1 tsp honey

⅔ cup tepid water

1 Grease a cookie sheet. Sift the flour into a large mixing bowl and stir in the husks remaining in the sifter.

2 Stir in the dried yeast, sage, and half of the sea salt. Reserve 1 teaspoon of the chopped garlic for sprinkling and stir the rest into the bowl. Add the honey with the tepid water and mix together to form a dough.

3 Turn the dough out on to a lightly floured counter and knead it for about 5 minutes (alternatively, use an electric mixer with a dough hook).

4 Place the dough in a greased bowl, cover, and let rise in a warm place until doubled in size.

3

6

cook's tip

Roll the dough into a long sausage and then curve it into a circular shape.

5

5 Knead the dough again for a few minutes, shape it into a circle (see Cook's Tip), and place on the cookie sheet.

6 Cover and let rise for an additional 30 minutes, or until springy to the touch. Sprinkle with the rest of the sea salt and garlic.

7 Bake in a preheated oven, 400°F, for 25–30 minutes. Let cool on a wire rack before serving.

mini rolls with sun-dried tomatoes

These white rolls have the addition of finely chopped sun-dried tomatoes.
The tomatoes are sold in jars and are readily available at most supermarkets.

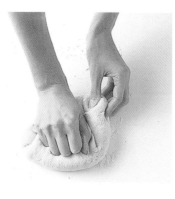

3

5

6

Makes 8

2 cups white bread flour

½ tsp salt

1 envelope rapid-rise dried yeast

¼ cup butter, melted and slightly cooled

3 tbsp milk, warmed

2 eggs, beaten

1¾ oz sun-dried tomatoes, well drained and
    finely chopped

milk, for brushing

1 Lightly grease a cookie sheet.

2 Sift the flour and salt into a large
mixing bowl. Stir in the yeast, then
pour in the butter, milk, and eggs. Mix
together to form a dough.

3 Turn the dough on to a lightly floured
counter and knead for about 5
minutes (alternatively, use an electric
mixer with a dough hook).

4 Place the dough in a greased bowl,
cover, and let rise in a warm place
for 1–1½ hours, or until the dough has
doubled in size. Punch down the dough
by kneading it for a few minutes.

5 Knead the sun-dried tomatoes into
the dough, sprinkling the work
counter with extra flour as the tomatoes
are quite oily.

6 Divide the dough into 8 balls and
place them on the cookie sheet.
Cover and let rise for about 30 minutes,
or until the rolls have doubled in size.

7 Brush the rolls with milk and bake in
a preheated oven, 450°F, for 10–15
minutes, or until the rolls are golden
brown.

8 Transfer the rolls to a wire rack and
let cool slightly before serving.

cook's tip

The rapid-rise dried yeast
used in this recipe is widely
available in most stores and
supermarkets.

mexican corn bread

This Mexican-style corn bread makes a great accompaniment
to a chile dish or it can be eaten on its own as a tasty snack.

3

Makes 12 bars

1 cup all-purpose flour

4½ oz polenta

1 tbsp baking powder

½ tsp salt

1 green chile, seeded and finely chopped

5 scallions, finely chopped

2 eggs

generous ½ cup sour cream

½ cup sunflower oil

variation

Add 4¹/₂ oz of corn kernels to the mixture in step 3, if you prefer.

4

1 Grease an 8-inch square cake pan and line the bottom with baking parchment.

2 In a large bowl, thoroughly mix together the flour, polenta, baking powder, and salt.

3 Add the finely chopped green chile and the scallions to the dry ingredients and mix well.

4 In a mixing pitcher, beat the eggs together with the sour cream and sunflower oil. Pour the mixture into the bowl of dry ingredients. Mix everything together quickly and thoroughly.

5 Pour the mixture into the prepared cake pan.

6 Bake in a preheated oven, 400°F, for 20–25 minutes, or until the loaf has risen and is lightly browned.

7 Let the bread cool slightly before turning out of the pan. Cut into bars or squares to serve.

4

spiced pumpkin bread

The pumpkin puree in this bread makes it beautifully moist.
This loaf is delicious eaten at any time of the day.

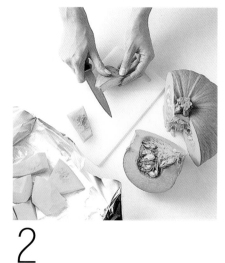

2

Serves 6-8

1 lb pumpkin flesh

½ cup butter, softened

¼ cup superfine sugar

2 eggs, beaten

2 cups all-purpose flour, sifted

1½ tsp baking powder

½ tsp salt

1 tsp ground allspice

1 oz pumpkin seeds

4

5

cook's tip

To ensure that the pumpkin puree is dry, place it in a pan over medium heat for a few minutes, stirring frequently, until it is thick.

1 Grease a 2-lb loaf pan with oil.

2 Chop the pumpkin into large pieces and wrap in buttered foil. Cook in a preheated oven, 400°F, for 30–40 minutes, or until tender.

3 Let the pumpkin cool completely before mashing well to make a thick puree.

4 In a bowl, cream the butter and sugar together until light and fluffy. Add the eggs a little at a time.

5 Stir in the pumpkin puree. Fold in the flour, baking powder, salt, and allspice.

6 Fold the pumpkin seeds gently through the mixture. Spoon the mixture into the loaf pan.

7 Bake in a preheated oven, 325°F, for about 1¼–1½ hours, or until a skewer inserted into the center of the bread comes out clean.

8 Let the bread cool and serve buttered, if desired.

spicy fruit loaf

This spicy, fruity bread is quick and easy to make. Serve it buttered and with a drizzle of honey for an afternoon snack.

Makes a 2-lb loaf

3 cups all-purpose flour

pinch of salt

1 tbsp baking powder

1 tbsp ground cinnamon

¾ cup butter, cut into small pieces

¾ cup soft brown sugar

¾ cup currants

finely grated rind of 1 orange

5–6 tbsp orange juice

6 tbsp milk

2 eggs, beaten lightly

1 Grease a 2-lb loaf pan and line the bottom smoothly with baking parchment.

2 Sift the flour, salt, baking powder, and ground cinnamon into a bowl. Then rub in the pieces of butter with your fingers, until the mixture resembles coarse bread crumbs.

3 Stir in the sugar, currants, and orange rind. Beat the orange juice, milk, and eggs together and add to the dry ingredients. Mix well together.

4 Spoon the mixture into the prepared pan. Make a slight dip in the middle of the mixture to help it rise evenly.

2

3

4

cook's tip

Once you have added the liquid to the dry ingredients, work as quickly as possible because the baking powder is activated by the liquid.

5 Bake in a preheated oven, 350°F, for about 60–70 minutes, or until a fine metal skewer inserted into the center of the loaf comes out clean.

6 Let the loaf cool before turning out of the pan. Transfer to a wire rack and let cool completely before slicing.

mango bread with golden raisins

This is a sweet bread that has pureed mango mixed into the dough, resulting in a moist loaf with an exotic flavor.

Makes 1 loaf

4 cups white bread flour

1 tsp salt

1 envelope rapid-rise dried yeast

1 tsp ground ginger

3 tbsp soft brown sugar

9 tsp butter, cut into small pieces

1 small mango, peeled, cored, and pureed

generous 1 cup tepid water

2 tbsp runny honey

¾ cup golden raisins

1 egg, beaten

confectioners' sugar, for dusting

1 Grease a cookie sheet. Sift the flour and salt into a large mixing bowl, then stir in the dried yeast, ground ginger, and brown sugar. Rub in the butter with your fingers.

2 Stir in the mango puree, water, and honey and mix together thoroughly to form a dough.

1

1

3 Place the dough on a lightly floured counter and knead for about 5 minutes, or until smooth (alternatively, use an electric mixer with a dough hook). Place the dough in a greased bowl, then cover, and let it rise in a warm place for about 1 hour, or until it has doubled in size.

4 Knead in the golden raisins and shape the dough into 2 sausage shapes, each 10 inches long. Carefully twist the 2 pieces together and pinch the ends to seal. Place the dough on the cookie sheet, then cover and let stand in a warm place for an additional 40 minutes.

5 Brush the loaf with the egg and bake in a preheated oven, 425°F, for 30 minutes, or until golden brown. Let cool on a wire rack. Dust with confectioners' sugar before serving.

2

cook's tip

You can tell when the bread is cooked, because it will sound hollow when tapped on the bottom.

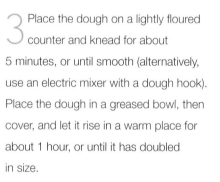

cheese & mustard bread

This tarty cheesy bread is ideal for a quick savory snack.
The mashed potato gives it a deliciously moist texture.

Makes 1 loaf

2 cups all-purpose flour

1 tsp salt

½ tsp mustard powder

2 tsp baking powder

4½ oz Leicester or colby cheese, grated

6 oz potatoes, cooked and mashed

¼ cup water

1 tbsp oil

cook's tip

You can use instant potato mix
for this bread, if desired.

variation

Add 1¾ oz chopped ham
to the mixture in step 3,
if you prefer.

3

4

1 Lightly grease a cookie sheet.

2 Sift the flour, salt, mustard powder,
and baking powder into a large
mixing bowl.

3 Reserve 2 tbsp of the grated cheese
and stir the rest into the bowl with
the cooked and mashed potatoes.

4 Pour in the water and the oil, and
stir all the ingredients together (the
mixture will be wet at this stage). Mix
them all to make a soft dough.

5 Turn out the dough on to a
floured counter and shape it into an
8-inch circle.

6 Place the round on the cookie sheet
and mark it into 4 portions with a
knife, without cutting through. Sprinkle
with the reserved cheese.

7 Bake in a preheated oven, 425°F, for
25–30 minutes.

8 Transfer the bread to a wire rack
and let cool. Serve the bread as
fresh as possible.

6

candied fruit wreath

This is a rich sweet bread combining alcohol, nuts, and fruit in a decorative wreath shape. It is ideal for serving at Thanksgiving. You can omit the frosting and glaze with 2 tablespoons honey, if preferred.

Makes 1 loaf

2 cups white bread flour

½ tsp salt

1 envelope rapid-rise dried yeast

6 tsp butter, cut into small pieces

½ cup tepid milk

1 egg, beaten

FILLING

1¾ oz butter, softened

3 tbsp soft brown sugar

1 oz chopped hazelnuts

1 oz candied ginger, chopped

1¾ oz candied citrus peel

1 tbsp rum or brandy

⅔ cup confectioners' sugar

2 tbsp lemon juice

1 Grease a cookie sheet. Sift the flour and salt into a bowl. Stir in the yeast. Rub in the butter with your fingers. Add the milk and egg and mix together to form a dough.

2 Place the dough in a greased bowl, cover, and let stand in a warm place for 40 minutes, or until doubled in size. Knead the dough lightly for 1 minute to punch down. Roll out to a rectangle measuring 12 x 9 inches.

2

3

3 To make the filling, cream together the butter and sugar until light and fluffy. Stir in the hazelnuts, ginger, candied peel, and rum or brandy. Spread the filling over the dough, leaving a 1-inch border.

4 Roll up the dough, starting from the long edge, to form a sausage shape. Cut into slices at 2-inch intervals and lay on the cookie sheet. Cover and let rise for 30 minutes.

5 Bake in a preheated oven, 325°F for 20–30 minutes, or until lightly golden. Meanwhile, mix the confectioners' sugar with enough lemon juice to form a thin frosting.

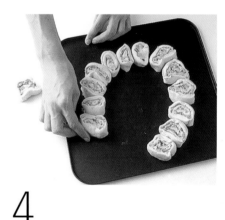

4

6 Let the loaf cool slightly before drizzling the whole circle with frosting. Let the frosting set slightly before serving the loaf.

chocolate loaf

For the chocoholics among us, this bread is great
fun to make and even better to eat.

Makes 1 loaf

4 cups white bread flour

¼ cup unsweetened cocoa

1 tsp salt

1 envelope rapid-rise dried yeast

6 tsp soft brown sugar

1 tbsp oil

1¼ cups tepid water

cook's tip

This bread can be sliced and
spread with butter or it can
be lightly toasted.

2

4

7

5 Place the dough on a lightly floured
counter and knead for 5 minutes.

6 Place the dough in a greased bowl,
then cover, and let rise in a warm
place for about 1 hour, or until the dough
has doubled in size.

7 Punch down the dough and shape
it into a loaf. Place the dough in the
prepared pan, then cover, and let rise
in a wam place for an additional
30 minutes.

8 Bake in a preheated oven, 400°F, for
25–30 minutes,or until a hollow
sound is heard when the bottom of the
bread is tapped.

9 Transfer the bread to a wire rack and
let cool. Cut into slices to serve.

1 Lightly grease a 2-lb loaf pan.

2 Sift the flour and unsweetened
cocoa into a large mixing bowl.

3 Stir in the salt, dried yeast, and
brown sugar.

4 Pour in the oil along with the
tepid water and mix the ingredients
together to make a dough.

mixed fruit, nut & cranberry loaf

The addition of chopped nuts, mixed peel, fresh orange juice, and dried cranberries makes this a rich, moist bread.

2

3

3

Serves 8-10

1½ cups self-rising flour

½ tsp baking powder

1 cup soft brown sugar

2 bananas, mashed

1¾ oz chopped mixed peel

1 oz chopped mixed nuts

1¾ oz dried cranberries

5–6 tbsp orange juice

2 eggs, beaten

⅔ cup sunflower oil

2¾ oz confectioners' sugar, sifted

grated rind of 1 orange

1 Grease a 2-lb loaf pan and line the base with baking parchment.

2 Sift the flour and baking powder into a large mixing bowl. Then stir in the sugar, bananas, chopped mixed peel, nuts, and cranberries.

3 Stir the orange juice, eggs, and oil together until well combined. Add the mixture to the dry ingredients and mix until well blended. Pour the mixture into the prepared pan.

4 Bake in a preheated oven, 350°F, for about 1 hour, until firm to the touch or until a fine skewer inserted into the center of the loaf comes out clean.

5 Turn out the loaf and let cool on a wire rack.

6 Mix the confectioners' sugar with a little water and drizzle the frosting over the loaf. Sprinkle the orange rind over the top. Let the frosting set before serving the loaf in slices.

cook's tip

This tea bread will keep for a couple of days. Wrap it carefully and store in a cool, dry place.

date & sesame loaf

This bread is full of good things—chopped dates, sesame seeds, and honey.
Toast thick slices and spread with soft cheese for a light snack.

Makes 1 loaf

1¼ cups white bread flour

¼ cup bread brown bread flour

½ tsp salt

1 envelope rapid-rise dried yeast

¾ cup tepid water

3 tbsp sunflower oil

3 tbsp honey

2¾ oz dates, chopped

2 tbsp sesame seeds

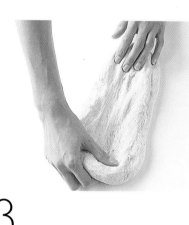

3

5

5

variation

Replace the sesame seeds
with sunflower seeds for a
slightly different texture,
if you prefer.

cook's tip

If you cannot find a warm
place, sit a bowl with the
dough in it over a pan of
warm water and cover.

1 Grease a 2-lb loaf pan. Sift the flours into a large mixing bowl, then stir in the salt and dried yeast.

2 Pour in the tepid water, oils, and honey. Mix everything together to form a dough.

3 Place the dough on a lightly floured counter and knead for about 5 minutes, or until smooth.

4 Place the dough in a greased bowl, then cover, and let rise in a warm place for about 1 hour, or until doubled in size.

5 Knead in the dates and sesame seeds. Shape the dough and place in the pan.

6 Cover and let stand in a warm place for an additional 30 minutes, or until springy to the touch.

7 Bake in a preheated oven, 425°F, for about 30 minutes, or until a hollow sound is heard when the bottom of the loaf is tapped.

8 Transfer the loaf to a wire rack and let cool. Serve cut into thick slices.

honeyed fruit bread

This delicious bread is excellent for an afternoon snack or coffee time with its moist texture and appealing flavor.

Serves 8-10

2 cups self-rising flour

¼ cup butter, cut into small pieces

¼ cup superfine sugar

4½ oz pitted dates, chopped

2 bananas, roughly mashed

2 eggs, lightly beaten

2 tbsp honey

1 Grease a 2-lb loaf pan and line the bottom with baking parchment.

2 Sift the flour into a mixing bowl.

3 Rub the butter into the flour with your fingertips until the mixture resembles fine bread crumbs.

4 Stir the sugar, chopped dates, bananas, beaten eggs, and honey into the dry ingredients. Mix together to form a soft dropping consistency.

5 Spoon the mixture into the prepared loaf pan and level the surface with the back of a knife.

4

4

5

6 Bake in a preheated oven, 325°F, for about 1 hour, or until golden and a fine metal skewer inserted into the center comes out clean.

7 Let the loaf cool in the pan before turning out and transferring to a wire rack.

8 Serve the loaf warm or cold, cut into thick slices.

cook's tip

This tea bread will keep for several days if stored in an airtight container and kept in a cool, dry place.

thyme puffs

These crescent-shaped snacks are very similar to croissants and are perfect for a quick and tasty bite to eat. They can also be shaped into twists, if preferred.

Makes 8

9 oz fresh ready-made puff pastry

⅛ cup butter, softened

1 garlic clove, minced

1 tsp lemon juice

1 tsp dried thyme

salt and pepper

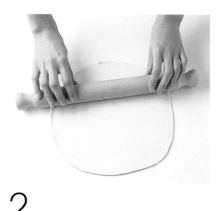

2

2

cook's tip

Dried herbs have a stronger flavor than fresh ones, which makes them perfect for these pastries. The puffs can be made with other dried herbs of your choice, such as rosemary and sage, or mixed herbs.

5

4 Spread a little of the butter and thyme mixture on to each wedge of pastry, dividing it equally between them.

5 Carefully roll up each wedge, starting from the wide end.

6 Arrange the puffs on the prepared cookie sheet and chill for about 30 minutes.

7 Moisten the cookie sheet with cold water. This will create a steamy atmosphere in the oven while the puffs are baking and help the pastries to rise.

8 Bake in a preheated oven, 400°F, for 10–15 minutes, or until the puffs are well risen and golden.

1 Lightly grease a cookie sheet.

2 On a lightly floured counter, roll out the pastry to form a 10-inch circle and cut into 8 wedges.

3 In a small bowl, mix the softened butter, garlic clove, lemon juice, and dried thyme together until soft. Season with salt and pepper to taste.

curried butter & parmesan crackers

When making these crackers, try different types of curry powder strengths until you find the one that suits your own taste.

3

Makes 40

¾ cup all-purpose flour

1 tsp salt

2 tsp curry powder

3½ oz mild hard cheese, grated

3½ oz Parmesan cheese, grated

⅓ cup butter, softened

cook's tip

These crackers can be stored for several days in an airtight metal or plastic container.

4

1 Lightly grease about 4 cookie sheets.

2 Sift the all-purpose flour and salt into a mixing bowl.

3 Stir in the curry powder and the grated mellow hard and Parmesan cheeses. Rub in the softened butter with your fingers until the mixture comes together to form a soft dough.

4 On a lightly floured counter, roll out the dough thinly to form a rectangle.

5 Using a 2-inch cookie cutter, cut out 40 round crackers.

5

6 Arrange the crackers on the prepared cookie sheets.

7 Bake in a preheated oven, 350°F, for 10–15 minutes.

8 Let the crackers cool slightly on the cookie sheets. Transfer the crackers to a wire rack until completely cold and crisp, then serve.

mini celery pies

These savory celery pies are quite irresistible, so it is probably a good idea to bake a double batch!

2

Makes 12

PASTRY

1 cup all-purpose flour

½ tsp salt

6 tsp butter, cut into small pieces

1 oz sharp cheese, grated

3–4 tbsp water

FILLING

10 tsp butter

4½ oz celery, finely chopped

2 garlic cloves, minced

1 small onion, finely chopped

1 tbsp all-purpose flour

¼ cup milk

salt

pinch of cayenne pepper

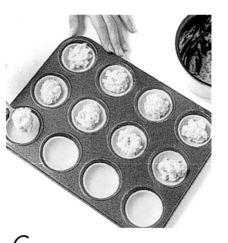

6

6

1 To make the filling, melt the butter in a skillet. Add the celery, garlic, and onion and cook gently for about 5 minutes, or until soft.

2 Reduce the heat and stir in the flour, then the milk. Bring back to a simmer, then heat gently until the mixture is thick, stirring frequently.

3 Season with salt and cayenne pepper. Let cool.

4 To make the pastry, sift the flour and salt into a mixing bowl and rub in the butter with your fingers. Stir the cheese into the mixture together with the cold water and mix to form a dough.

5 Roll out three-fourths of the dough on to a lightly floured counter. Using a 2½-inch cookie cutter, cut out 12 circles. Line a muffin pan with the circles.

6 Divide the filling between the pastry rounds. Roll out the remaining dough and, using a 2-inch cutter, cut out 12 circles. Place the smaller circles on top of the pie filling and seal well. Make a slit in each pie and let chill for 30 minutes.

7 Bake in a preheated oven, 425°F, for 15–20 minutes. Let cool in the pan for about 10 minutes before turning out. Serve warm.

dairy-free vegetable pasties

These pasties, which are suitable for vegans, are a delicious combination of vegetables and spices. They can be eaten either hot or cold.

Makes 4

1¾ cups all-purpose whole-wheat flour

½ cup vegan margarine, cut into small pieces

4 tbsp water

2 tbsp oil

8 oz diced root vegetables (potatoes, carrots, and parsnips or rutabagas)

1 small onion, chopped

2 garlic cloves, finely chopped

½ tsp curry powder

½ tsp ground turmeric

½ tsp ground cumin

½ tsp whole-grain mustard

5 tbsp vegetable bouillon

soy milk, to glaze

cook's tip

The vegetable filling can be made in advance and stored in the refrigerator until required.

1

2

5

1 Place the flour in a mixing bowl and rub in the vegan margarine with your fingertips until the mixture resembles bread crumbs. Stir in the water and bring together to form a soft dough. Wrap and let chill in the refrigerator for 30 minutes.

2 To make the filling, heat the oil in a large pan. Add the diced root vegetables, chopped onion, and garlic. Cook for 2 minutes, then stir in all the spices and the mustard, turning the vegetables to coat them. Cook the vegetables for an additional 1 minute.

3 Add the bouillon to the pan and bring to a boil. Cover and simmer for about 20 minutes, stirring occasionally, until the vegetables are tender and the liquid has been absorbed. Let cool.

4 Divide the pastry into 4 portions. Roll each portion into a 6-inch circle. Place the filling on one half of each circle.

5 Brush the edges of each round with soy milk, then fold over and press the edges together to seal. Place on a cookie sheet. Bake in a preheated oven, 400°F, for 25–30 minutes, or until the pastry is golden brown.

potato & red onion pie

This pie with its rich filling is a great alternative to serving potatoes as a side dish with any meal. Alternatively, serve with salad for a light lunch.

Serves 6

1 lb 9 oz potatoes, peeled and
   thinly sliced

2 scallions, finely chopped

1 red onion, finely chopped

⅔ cup heavy cream

1 lb fresh ready-made puff pastry

2 eggs, beaten

salt and pepper

2

4

1 Lightly grease a cookie sheet. Bring a pan of water to a boil, then add the sliced potatoes. Bring back to a boil and simmer for a few minutes. Drain the potato slices and let cool. Dry off any excess moisture with paper towels.

2 In a bowl, mix together the scallions, red onion, and the cooled potato

slices. Stir in 2 tbsp of the cream and plenty of seasoning.

3 Divide the pastry in half and roll out one piece to a 9-inch circle. Roll the remaining pastry to a 10-inch circle.

4 Place the smaller circle on to the cookie sheet and top with the potato mixture, leaving a 1-inch border. Brush this border with a little of the beaten egg.

5 Top with the larger circle of pastry, seal well, and crimp the edges of the pastry. Cut a steam vent in the middle of the pastry and mark with a pattern. Brush with the beaten egg and bake in a preheated oven, 400°F, for 30 minutes.

6 Mix the remaining beaten egg with the rest of the cream and pour into the pie through the steam vent. Return to the oven for 15 minutes, then let cool for 30 minutes. Serve warm or cold.

cook's tip

The filling may be prepared up to 4 hours in advance.

dairy-free mushroom pie

The whole mushrooms give this wholesome vegan pie a wonderful
aromatic flavor. The pie can be frozen uncooked and baked from frozen.

Serves 4-6

PASTRY

1¾ cups plain whole-wheat flour

⅓ cup vegan margarine, cut into small pieces

4 tbsp water

soy milk, to glaze

FILLING

6 tsp vegan margarine

1 onion, chopped

1 garlic clove, chopped finely

4½ oz small mushrooms, sliced

1 tbsp all-purpose flour

⅔ cup vegetable bouillon

1 tbsp tomato paste

6 oz brazil nuts, chopped

2¼ oz fresh whole-wheat bread crumbs

2 tbsp chopped fresh parsley

½ tsp pepper

1 To make the pastry, place the flour in a mixing bowl and rub in the vegan margarine with your fingertips until the mixture resembles fine bread crumbs. Stir in the water and bring together to form a dough. Wrap and chill for 30 minutes.

2

2

2

2 To make the filling, melt half of the margarine in a skillet. Add the onion, garlic, and mushrooms and cook for 5 minutes, until soft. Add the flour and cook for 1 minute, stirring frequently. Gradually add the bouillon, stirring until the sauce is smooth and beginning to thicken. Stir in the tomato paste, brazil nuts, bread crumbs, parsley, and pepper. Let cool slightly.

3 On a lightly floured counter, roll out two-thirds of the pastry and use to line an 8-inch loose-bottomed tart pan or pie dish. Spread the filling in the pie shell. Brush the edges of the pastry with soy milk. Roll out the remaining pastry to fit the top of the pie. Seal the edges, then make a slit in the top of the pastry and brush with soy milk.

4 Bake the pie in a preheated oven, 400°F, for 30–40 minutes, or until golden brown.

cheese, garlic & parsley pies

These crisp pies are filled with a tasty onion, garlic, and parsley mixture, making them ideal for lunch boxes.

1

1

Makes 4

3 tbsp vegetable oil

4 onions, peeled and finely sliced

4 garlic cloves, minced

4 tbsp finely chopped fresh
  parsley

2¾ oz sharp cheese, grated

salt and pepper

PASTRY

1½ cups all-purpose flour

½ tsp salt

⅓ cup butter, cut into small pieces

3–4 tbsp water

5

cook's tip

You can prepare the onion filling in advance and then store it in the refrigerator until required.

1 Heat the oil in a skillet. Add the onions and garlic and cook for 10–15 minutes, or until the onions are soft. Remove the skillet from the heat, stir in the parsley and cheese, and season to taste.

2 To make the pastry, sift the flour and salt into a mixing bowl and rub in the butter with your fingertips until the mixture resembles bread crumbs. Stir in the water and mix to a dough.

3 On a lightly floured counter, roll out the dough and then divide it into 8 portions.

4 Roll out each portion to a 4-inch circle and use half of the rounds to line 4 individual tart pans.

5 Fill each round with one fourth of the onion mixture. Cover with the remaining 4 pastry circles. Make a slit in the top of each tart with the point of a knife and seal the edges with the back of a teaspoon.

6 Bake in a preheated oven, 425°F, for 20 minutes. Serve hot or cold.

ham & parmesan pies with chives

These attractive lattice pies are equally delicious served hot or cold.
They make a good picnic food served with salad.

Makes 6

9 oz fresh ready-made puff pastry

1¾ oz ham, finely chopped

4½ oz full-fat soft cheese

2 tbsp chopped fresh chives

1 egg, beaten

2 tbsp freshly grated Parmesan cheese

pepper

3

1 Roll out the pastry thinly on to a lightly floured work counter. Cut out 12 rectangles measuring 6 x 2 inches.

2 Place the rectangles on to greased cookie sheets and let chill in the refrigerator for 30 minutes.

3 Meanwhile, combine the ham, cheese, and chives in a small bowl. Season with pepper to taste.

4 Spread the ham and cheese mixture along the center of 6 of the rectangles, leaving a 1-inch border around each one. Brush the border with the beaten egg.

5 To make the lattice pattern, fold the remaining rectangles lengthwise. Leaving a 1-inch border, cut vertical lines across one edge of the rectangles.

6 Unfold the rectangles and place them over the rectangles topped with the ham and cheese mixture set on the cookie sheets. Seal the pastry edges well and lightly sprinkle with the Parmesan cheese.

7 Bake in a preheated oven, 350°F, for 15–20 minutes. Serve hot or cold.

4

5

cook's tip

These pies can be made in advance, frozen uncooked and baked fresh when required.

savory tomato pastries

These tomato-flavored pastries should be eaten as fresh as possible to enjoy the crisp buttery puff pastry.

Serves 6

9 oz fresh ready-made puff pastry

1 egg, beaten

2 tbsp pesto

6 plum tomatoes, sliced

salt and pepper

fresh thyme leaves, to garnish (optional)

1 On a lightly floured counter, roll out the pastry to an area measuring 12 x 10 inches.

2 Cut the rectangle in half and divide each half into 3 pieces to make 6 even-size rectangles. Let chill for 20 minutes.

3 Lightly score the edges of the pastry rectangles and brush with the beaten egg.

3

4

4 Spread the pesto over the rectangles, dividing it equally between them, leaving a 1-inch border on each one.

5 Arrange the tomato slices along the center of each rectangle on top of the pesto.

6 Season well with salt and pepper to taste and lightly sprinkle with fresh thyme leaves, if using.

7 Bake in a preheated oven, 400°F, for 15–20 minutes, or until well risen and golden brown.

8 Transfer the tomato tarts to warm serving plates straight from the oven and serve while they are still very hot.

5

variation

Instead of individual tarts, roll the pastry out to form 1 large rectangle. Spoon over the pesto and arrange the tomatoes over the top.

French pissaladière with marjoram

This is a variation of the classic Italian pizza, but it is made with ready-made puff pastry. It is perfect for outdoor eating.

Serves 8

4 tbsp olive oil

1 lb 9 oz red onions, thinly sliced

2 garlic cloves, minced

2 tsp superfine sugar

2 tbsp red wine vinegar

12 oz fresh ready-made puff pastry

salt and pepper

TOPPING

1¾ oz canned anchovy fillets

12 green pitted olives

1 tsp dried marjoram

variation

Cut the pissaladière into squares or triangles for easy finger food at a party or outdoor buffet.

2

3

5

3 On a lightly floured counter, roll out the pastry to a rectangle about 13 x 9 inches. Place the pastry rectangle on to the prepared pan, pushing the pastry well into the corners of the pan.

4 Spread the onion mixture evenly over the pastry.

5 Arrange the anchovy fillets and green olives on top, then sprinkle with the dried marjoram.

6 Bake in a preheated oven, 425°F, for about 20-25 minutes, or until the pissaladière is lightly golden. Serve very hot, straight from the oven.

1 Lightly grease a jelly-roll pan. Heat the olive oil in a large pan. Add the onions and garlic and then cook over a low heat for about 30 minutes, stirring occasionally.

2 Add the sugar and red wine vinegar to the pan and season with plenty of salt and pepper.

zucchini & mixed bell pepper flan

This tart is full of color and flavor from the zucchini and red
and green bell peppers. It makes a great change from a quiche Lorraine.

Serves 6-8

9 oz ready-made fresh puff pastry

3 tbsp olive oil

2 red bell peppers, seeded and diced

2 green bell peppers, seeded
  and diced

⅔ cup heavy cream

1 egg

2 zucchini, sliced

salt and pepper

cook's tip

This recipe could be used to
make 6 individual tarts—use
·6 x 4 inch pans and bake them
for 20 minutes.

1

2

6

1 Roll out the pastry on a lightly floured counter and line an 8-inch loose-bottomed tart pan. Let chill in the refrigerator for 20 minutes.

2 Meanwhile, heat 2 tbsp of the olive oil in a pan and cook the bell peppers for about 8 minutes, or until softened, stirring frequently.

3 Whisk the heavy cream and egg together in a bowl and season to taste with salt and pepper. Stir in the cooked bell peppers.

4 Heat the remaining oil in a pan and cook the zucchini slices for 4–5 minutes, or until lightly browned.

5 Pour the egg and bell pepper mixture into the pie shell.

6 Arrange the zucchini slices around the edge of the tart.

7 Bake in a preheated oven, 350°F, for 35–40 minutes, or until just set and golden brown.

dairy-free lentil, onion & parsley tart

This savory tart combines lentils and red bell peppers in a tasty whole-wheat pie shell. This tart is suitable for vegans.

Serves 6-8

PASTRY

1¾ cups plain whole-wheat flour

⅓ cup vegan margarine, cut into small pieces

4 tbsp water

FILLING

6 oz red lentils, rinsed

1¼ cups vegetable bouillon

3 tsp vegan margarine

1 onion, chopped

2 red bell peppers, cored, seeded, and diced

1 tsp yeast extract

1 tbsp tomato paste

3 tbsp chopped fresh parsley

pepper

1

2

4

variation

Add corn to the tart in step 4 for a colorful and tasty change.

1 To make the pastry, place the flour in a mixing bowl and rub in the vegan margarine with your fingertips, until the mixture resembles fine bread crumbs. Stir in the water and bring together to form a dough. Wrap and chill for 30 minutes.

2 Meanwhile, make the filling. Put the lentils in a pan with the bouillon and bring to a boil. Simmer for 10 minutes, or until the lentils are tender and can be mashed to a purée.

3 Melt the margarine in a small pan. Add the chopped onion and diced red bell peppers and cook until just soft.

4 Add the lentil puree, yeast extract, tomato paste, and parsley. Season with pepper. Mix until well combined.

5 On a lightly floured counter, roll out the dough and line a 9½-inch loose-bottomed tart pan. Prick the bottom of the pastry with a fork and spoon the lentil mixture into the pie shell.

6 Bake in a preheated oven, 400°F, for 30 minutes, or until the filling is firm.

creamy red onion & asparagus tart

Fresh asparagus is now readily available all year round,
so you can make this tasty supper dish at any time.

Serves 6

9 oz fresh ready-made
   shortcrust pastry

9 oz asparagus

1 tbsp vegetable oil

1 red onion, chopped finely

1 oz hazelnuts, chopped

7 oz goat cheese

2 eggs, beaten

4 tbsp light cream

salt and pepper

1 On a lightly floured counter, roll out the pastry and line a 9½-inch loose-bottomed tart pan. Prick the bottom of the pastry with a fork and let chill for 30 minutes.

2 Line the pie shell with foil and baking beans and bake in a preheated oven, 375°F, for about 15 minutes.

2

4

3 Remove the foil and baking beans and cook for another 15 minutes.

4 Cook the asparagus in boiling water for 2–3 minutes, drain, and cut into bite-size pieces.

5 Heat the oil in a small skillet and cook the onion until soft and lightly golden. Spoon the asparagus, onion, and hazelnuts into the prepared pie shell.

6 Beat together the cheese, eggs, and cream until smooth, or process in a blender until smooth. Season well with salt and pepper, then pour the mixture over the asparagus, onion, and hazelnuts.

6

7 Bake in the oven for 15–20 minutes, or until the cheese filling is just set. Serve warm or cold.

variation

Omit the hazelnuts and sprinkle Parmesan cheese over the top of the tart just before cooking in the oven, if you prefer.

bacon, onion & parmesan tart

This crisp pie shell is filled with onions and
cheese and baked until it melts in the mouth.

2

3

5

Serves 6

9 oz fresh ready-made unsweetened pastry

8 tsp butter

2¾ oz bacon, chopped

1lb 9 oz onions, peeled and thinly sliced

2 eggs, beaten

1¾ oz Parmesan cheese, grated

1 tsp dried sage

salt and pepper

1 Roll out the pastry on a lightly floured
counter and line a 9½-inch loose-
bottomed tart pan.

2 Prick the bottom of the pastry with a
fork and let chill for 30 minutes.

3 Heat the butter in a pan, add the
chopped bacon and sliced onions,
and sweat them over a low heat for
about 25 minutes, or until tender. If the
onion slices start to brown, add 1 tbsp
water to the pan.

4 Add the beaten eggs to the onion
mixture and stir in the cheese, sage,
and salt and pepper to taste.

5 Spoon the onion mixture into the
prepared pie shell.

6 Bake in a preheated oven, 350°F, for
20-30 minutes, or until the tart has
just set.

7 Let cool slightly in the pan, then
serve the tart warm or cold.

variation

For a vegetarian version of
this tart, replace the bacon
with the same amount of
chopped mushrooms.

red onion & thyme tart

Ready-made puff pastry works extremely well in this recipe
and means you can create a quick savory tart in very little time.

2

Serves 4

10 tsp butter

6 tsp sugar

1 lb red onions, peeled and cut into fourths

3 tbsp red wine vinegar

2 tbsp fresh thyme leaves

8 oz fresh ready-made puff pastry

salt and pepper

3

1   Place the butter and sugar in a 9-inch ovenproof skillet and cook over a medium heat until melted.

2   Add the red onion pieces and sweat them over low heat for 10–15 minutes, or until golden, stirring occasionally.

3   Add the red wine vinegar and thyme leaves to the pan. Season with salt and pepper, then simmer over a medium heat until the liquid has reduced and the red onion is coated in sauce.

4   On a lightly floured counter, roll out the pastry to a circle slightly larger than the skillet.

5   Place the pastry over the onion mixture and press down, tucking in the edges to seal the pastry.

5

6   Bake in a preheated oven, 350°F, for 20-25 minutes. Let the tart stand for 10 minutes.

7   To turn out, place a serving plate over the skillet and carefully invert them both so that the pastry becomes the bottom of the tart. Serve the tart warm.

variation

Replace the red onions with shallots, leaving them whole, if you prefer.

cheese & onion tartlets

Serve these delicious little savory tarts as finger food at buffets or drinks parties.

Serves 12

PASTRY

1 cup all-purpose flour

¼ tsp salt

½ cup butter, cut into small pieces

1–2 tbsp water

FILLING

1 egg, beaten

generous ½ cup light cream

1¾ oz Leicester or colby cheese, grated

3 scallions, finely chopped

salt

cayenne pepper

2

3

1 To make the pastry, sift the flour and salt into a mixing bowl. Rub in the butter with your fingers until the mixture resembles bread crumbs. Stir in the water and mix to form a dough.

2 Roll out the pastry on to a lightly floured counter. Using a 3-inch cookie cutter, stamp out 12 circles from the pastry and line a muffin pan.

4

3 To make the filling, whisk together the beaten egg, light cream, grated cheese, and chopped scallions in a mixing pitcher. Season to taste with salt and cayenne pepper.

4 Pour the filling mixture into the pie shells and bake in a preheated oven, 350°F, for about 20–25 minutes, or until the filling is just set. Serve the tartlets warm or cold.

variation

Top each tartlet with slices of fresh tomato before baking, if you prefer.

There is nothing quite as nice as home-made chocolates and candies—they leave the average box of ready-made candies in the shade! You'll find recipes in this chapter to suit everybody's taste. Wonderful, rich, melt-in-the-mouth chocolate truffles, crispy florentines, nutty chocolate creams, and rich chocolate liqueurs—they're all here. There is even some simple-to-make chocolate fudge, so there is no need to fiddle about with candy thermometers.

Looking for something to wash it all down? We have included two delightfully cool summer chocolate drinks that will simply put ready-made chocolate drinks to shame. Enjoy!

candies & drinks for every occasion

rum & coconut truffles

Truffles are always popular. They make a fabulous gift or, served with coffee, they are a perfect end to a meal.

Makes about 20

5½ oz dark chocolate

small knob of butter

2 tbsp rum

1¼ oz shredded coconut

3½ oz cake crumbs

6 tbsp confectioners' sugar

2 tbsp unsweetened cocoa

2

3

4

variation

Make the truffles with white chocolate and replace the rum with coconut liqueur or milk, if you prefer. Roll them in unsweetened cocoa or dip in melted milk chocolate.

cook's tip

These truffles will keep for about 2 weeks in a cool place.

1 Break the chocolate into pieces and place in a bowl with the butter. Set the bowl over a pan of gently simmering water, then stir until melted and thoroughly combined.

2 Remove from the heat and beat in the rum. Stir in the shredded coconut, cake crumbs, and 1¼ oz of the confectioners' sugar. Beat until combined. Add a little extra rum if the mixture is stiff.

3 Roll the mixture into small balls and place them on a sheet of baking parchment. Let chill until firm.

4 Sift the remaining confectioners' sugar on to a large plate. Sift the unsweetened cocoa on to another plate. Roll half of the truffles in the confectioners' sugar until coated, and then roll the remaining truffles in the unsweetened cocoa.

5 Place the truffles in paper candy cases and let chill until required.

chocolate cherry & nut liqueurs

These tasty chocolate cups are filled with a delicious liqueur-flavored filling. They are a little fiddly to make, but lots of fun! Use your favourite liqueur to flavor the cream.

Makes 20

3½ oz dark chocolate

about 5 candied cherries, halved

about 10 hazelnuts or macadamia nuts

⅔ cup heavy cream

2 tbsp confectioners' sugar

4 tbsps liqueur

TO FINISH

1¾ oz dark chocolate, melted

a little melted white chocolate, or white
    chocolate curls (see page 50), or extra
    nuts and cherries

cook's tip

Candy cases can vary in size. Use the smallest you can find for this recipe.

5

5

1 Line a cookie sheet with a sheet of baking parchment. Melt the chocolate and spoon it into 20 paper candy cases, spreading up the sides with a small spoon or pastry brush. Place upside down on the prepared cookie sheet and let set.

2 Carefully peel away the paper cases. Place a cherry or nut in the base of each cup.

3 To make the filling, place the heavy cream in a mixing bowl and sift the confectioners' sugar on top. Whisk the cream until it is just holding its shape, then whisk in the liqueur.

4 Place the cream in a pastry bag fitted with a ½-inch plain tip and pipe a little into each chocolate case. Let chill for 20 minutes.

5

5 To finish, spoon the melted dark chocolate over the cream to cover it and pipe the melted white chocolate on top, swirling it into the dark chocolate with a toothpick. Let harden. Alternatively, cover the cream with the melted dark chocolate and decorate with white chocolate curls before setting. Or, place a small piece of nut or cherry on top of the cream and then cover with dark chocolate.

chocolate orange cups

A creamy, orange-flavored chocolate filling in white chocolate cups makes a wonderful treat.

Makes 20

3½ oz white chocolate

FILLING

5½ oz orange-flavored dark chocolate

⅔ cup heavy cream

2 tbsp confectioners' sugar

cook's tip

If they do not hold their shape well, use 2 cases to make a double-thickness mold. Foil cases are firmer, so use these if you can find them.

cook's tip

Use the smallest candy cases you can find for these cups.

2

1 Line a cookie sheet with a sheet of baking parchment. Melt the chocolate and spoon it into 20 paper candy cases, spreading up the sides with a small spoon or pastry brush. Place upside down on the prepared cookie sheet and let set.

2 When set, carefully peel away the paper cases.

3 To make the filling, melt the orange-flavored chocolate and place in a mixing bowl with the heavy cream and the confectioners' sugar. Beat until smooth. Chill until the mixture becomes firm enough to pipe, stirring occasionally.

4 Place the filling in a pastry bag fitted with a star tip and pipe a little into each case. Let chill until required.

3

4

variation

Add 1 tbsp orange-flavored liqueur to the filling, if preferred.

chocolate almond truffles

These tasty little morsels are simplicity itself to make. Served with coffee, they make the perfect finale to a meal.

Makes about 24

6 oz dark chocolate

2 tbsp almond-flavored liqueur or orange-
    flavored liqueur

3 tbsp unsalted butter

1¾ oz confectioners' sugar

½ cup ground almonds

1¾ oz grated chocolate

2

2

cook's tip

These truffles will keep for about 2 weeks in a cool place.

variation

For a sweeter truffle, use milk chocolate instead of dark chocolate. Dip the truffles in melted chocolate to finish, if desired.

4

variation

The almond-flavored liqueur gives these truffles an authentic Italian flavor. The original almond liqueur, Amaretto di Saronno, comes from Saronno in Italy.

1 Melt the dark chocolate with the liqueur in a bowl set over a pan of hot water, stirring until well combined.

2 Add the butter and stir until it has melted. Stir in the confectioners' sugar and the ground almonds.

3 Let the mixture stand in a cool place until firm enough to roll into about 24 balls.

4 Place the grated chocolate on a plate and roll the truffles in the chocolate to coat them.

5 Place the truffles in paper candy cases and chill.

cherry & marzipan chocolates

These tasty cherry and marzipan candies are simple to make. Serve as petits fours at the end of a meal or for an indulgent nibble at any time of the day.

Serves 4

12 candied cherries

2 tbsp rum or brandy

9 oz marzipan

5½ oz dark chocolate

extra milk, dark, or white chocolate, to
    decorate (optional)

variation

Use a whole almond in place
of the halved candied cherries
and omit the rum or brandy.

variation

Flatten the marzipan and use
it to mold around the cherries
to cover them, then dip in the
chocolate as above.

1 Line a cookie sheet smoothly with a sheet of baking parchment.

2 Cut the cherries in half and place in a small bowl. Add the rum or brandy and stir to coat. Let the cherries soak for at least 1 hour, stirring occasionally.

3 Divide the marzipan into 24 pieces and roll each piece into a ball. Press half a cherry into the top of each marzipan ball.

4 Break the chocolate into pieces, then place in a bowl and set over a pan of hot water. Stir until the chocolate has melted.

5 Dip each candy into the melted chocolate, letting the excess drip back into the bowl. Place the coated cherries on the baking parchment and chill until set.

6 If liked, melt a little extra chocolate and drizzle it over the top of the coated cherries. Let them set.

creamy white truffles

These delicious creamy truffles will testify to the fact that there is nothing quite as nice as home-made chocolates. It is worth buying the best chocolate you can for these truffles.

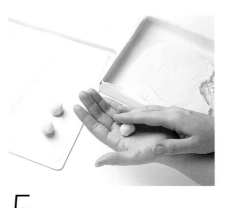

4

Makes about 20

2 tbsp unsalted butter

5 tbsp heavy cream

8 oz good-quality Swiss white chocolate

1 tbsp orange-flavored liqueur (optional)

TO FINISH

3½ oz white chocolate

1 Line a jelly roll pan with baking parchment.

2 Place the butter and cream in a small pan and bring slowly to a boil, stirring constantly. Boil for 1 minute, then remove from the heat.

3 Break the chocolate into pieces and add to the cream. Stir until melted, then beat in the liqueur, if using.

5

4 Pour into the prepared pan and chill for about 2 hours, or until firm.

5 Break off pieces of mixture and roll them into balls. Chill for an additional 30 minutes before finishing the truffles.

6 To finish, melt the white chocolate. Dip the balls in the chocolate, letting the excess drip back into the bowl. Place on non-stick baking parchment and swirl the chocolate with the prongs of a fork. Let harden.

7 Drizzle a little melted dark chocolate over the truffles if you wish and let them set. Place the truffles in paper cases to serve.

cook's tip

The chocolates can be kept in the refrigerator for up to 2 weeks.

6

cook's tip

The truffle mixture needs to be firm, but not too hard to roll. If the mixture is too hard, let it stand at room temperature for a few minutes to soften slightly. During rolling, the mixture will become sticky, but it will reharden in the refrigerator before coating.

chocolate mint horns

These unusual cone-shaped chocolates are filled with a mint-flavored cream, and are perfect for an after-dinner treat.

Makes 10

2¾ oz dark chocolate

⅓ cup heavy cream

1 tbsp confectioners' sugar

1 tbsp crème de menthe

chocolate coffee beans, to decorate

   (optional)

1 Cut ten 3-inch circles of baking parchment. Shape each circle into a cone shape and secure with sticky tape.

2 Melt the chocolate. Using a small pastry brush or clean artists' brush, brush the inside of each cone with melted chocolate.

3 Brush a second layer of chocolate on the inside of the cones and let them chill until set. Carefully peel away the parchment.

4 Place the heavy cream, confectioners' sugar, and crème de menthe in a mixing bowl and whip until just holding its shape. Place in a pastry bag fitted with a star tip and pipe the mixture into the chocolate cones.

5 Decorate the cones with chocolate coffee beans (if using) and then chill until required.

1

2

3

variation

Use a different flavored liqueur to flavor the cream: a coffee-flavored liqueur is perfect. If you want a mint flavor without using a liqueur, use a few drops of peppermint extract to flavor the cream according to taste.

cook's tip

The chocolate cones can be made in advance and kept in the refrigerator for up to 1 week. Do not fill them more than 2 hours before you are going to serve them.

crispy chocolate bites

Nuts and crisp cookies encased in chocolate make
these candies rich, crisp, and quite irresistible!

Makes about 30

6 oz white chocolate

3½ oz graham crackers

3½ oz macadamia nuts or brazil nuts,
   chopped

1 oz fresh ginger, chopped (optional)

6 oz dark chocolate

1 Line a cookie sheet with a sheet of
baking parchment. Break the white
chocolate into small pieces and place in
a large mixing bowl set over a pan of
gently simmering water; stir until melted.

2 Break the graham crackers into
small pieces. Stir the graham
crackers into the melted chocolate
with the chopped nuts and fresh ginger,
if using.

3 Place heaped teaspoons of the
mixture on to the prepared
cookie sheet.

2

3

5

4 Chill the mixture until set, then
carefully remove the clusters from
the baking parchment.

5 Melt the dark chocolate and let it
cool slightly. Dip the clusters into the
melted chocolate, letting the excess drip
back into the bowl. Return the clusters to
the cookie sheet and chill in the
refrigerator until set.

cook's tip

The clusters can be stored
for up to 1 week in a cool,
dry place.

cook's tip

Macadamia and brazil nuts are
both rich and high in fat,
which makes them particularly
popular for confectionery, but
other nuts can be used, if
preferred.

chocolate vanilla cups

Mascarpone—the velvety smooth Italian cheese—makes a rich, creamy filling for these tasty chocolates.

Makes 20

3½ oz dark chocolate

FILLING

3½ oz milk or dark chocolate

7 oz mascarpone cheese

¼ tsp vanilla extract

unsweetened cocoa, to dust

variation

You can use lightly whipped heavy cream instead of the mascarpone cheese, if preferred.

cook's tip

Mascarpone is a rich Italian soft cheese made from fresh cream, so it has a high fat content. Its delicate flavor blends well with chocolate.

1

3

4

2 When set, carefully peel away the paper cases.

3 To make the filling, melt the dark or milk chocolate. Place the mascarpone cheese in a bowl and beat in the vanilla extract and melted chocolate and beat until well combined. Let the mixture chill, beating occasionally until firm enough to pipe.

4 Place the mascarpone filling in a pastry bag fitted with a star tip and pipe the mixture into the cups. Decorate with a dusting of unsweetened cocoa.

1 Line a cookie sheet with a sheet of baking parchment. Melt the chocolate and spoon it into 20 paper candy cases, spreading up the sides with a small spoon or pastry brush. Place upside down on the prepared cookie sheet and let set.

cherry & apricot morsels

These delightful little morsels make the perfect gift, if you can resist eating them all yourself!

2

Makes about 30

1 lb marzipan

⅓ cup candied cherries, very finelychopped

1 oz fresh ginger, very finely chopped

1¼ oz no-soak dried apricots, very finely chopped

12 oz dark chocolate

1 oz white chocolate

confectioners' sugar, to dust

5

6

3 Do the same with the fresh ginger and another portion of marzipan and then with the apricots and the third portion of marzipan.

4 Form each flavored portion of marzipan into small balls, ensuring you keep the different flavors separate.

5 Melt the dark chocolate. Dip one of each flavored ball of marzipan into the chocolate by spiking each one with a toothpick, letting the excess chocolate drip back into the bowl.

6 Carefully place the balls in clusters of the three flavors on the prepared cookie sheet. Repeat with the remaining marzipan balls. Chill until set.

7 Melt the white chocolate and drizzle a little over the tops of each cluster of marzipan balls. Chill until hardened, then remove from the baking parchment and dust with sugar to serve.

variation

Coat the marzipan balls in white or milk chocolate and drizzle with dark chocolate, if you prefer.

1 Line a cookie sheet with a sheet of baking parchment. Divide the marzipan into 3 balls and knead each ball to soften it.

2 Work the candied cherries into one portion of the marzipan by kneading on a counter lightly dusted with confectioners' sugar.

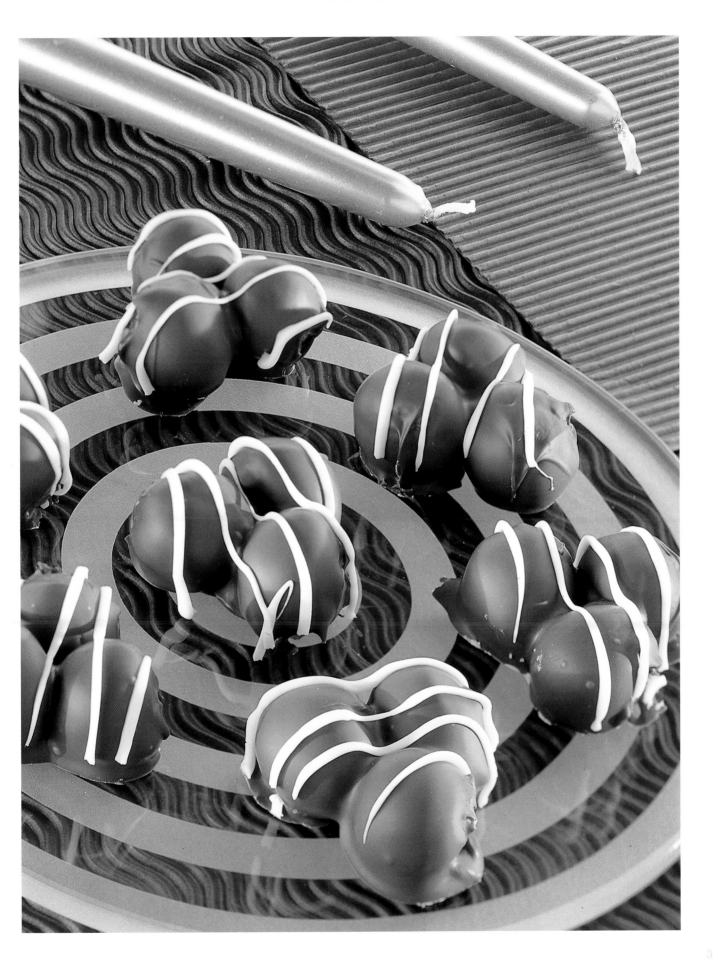

chewy chocolate clusters

Young children will love these chewy bites. You can vary the ingredients and use different nuts and dried fruits according to taste.

Makes 18

4½ oz milk chocolate

2½ oz multi-colored mini marshmallows

¼ cup chopped walnuts

1 oz no-soak apricots, chopped

2

variation

Light, fluffy marshmallows are available in white or pastel colors. If you cannot find mini marshmallows, use large ones and snip them into smaller pieces with kitchen scissors before mixing them into the melted chocolate in step 3.

cook's tip

These candies can be stored in a cool, dry place for up to 2 weeks.

1 Line a cookie sheet with baking parchment and set aside.

2 Break the milk chocolate into small pieces and place in a large mixing bowl. Set the bowl over a pan of simmering water and stir until the chocolate has melted.

3

3 Stir in the marshmallows, walnuts, and apricots and toss in the melted chocolate until well covered.

4 Place heaped teaspoons of the mixture on to the prepared cookie sheet.

4

5 Let the candies chill in the refrigerator until set.

6 Once they are firmly set, carefully remove the candies from the baking parchment.

7 The chewy bites can be placed in paper candy cases to serve them, if desired.

mini chocolate pies

These small pie shells are filled with a rich chocolate filling to serve as petits fours. Use mini muffin pans or small individual tartlet pans to make the pie shells.

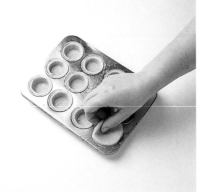

2

Serves 4

1½ cups all-purpose flour

¼ cup butter

1 tbsp superfine sugar

about 1 tbsp water

FILLING

3½ oz full-fat soft cheese

5 tsp superfine sugar

1 small egg, lightly beaten

1¾ oz dark chocolate

TO DECORATE

⅔ cup heavy cream

dark chocolate curls (see page 50)

unsweetened cocoa, to dust

3

4

2 Roll out the pastry on a lightly floured counter and use to line 18 mini tartlet pans or mini muffin pans. Prick the bases with a toothpick.

3 Beat together the full-fat soft cheese and the sugar. Beat in the egg. Melt the chocolate and beat it into the mixture. Spoon into the pie shells and bake in a preheated oven, 375°F, for 15 minutes, or until the pastry is crisp and the filling set. Place the pans on a wire rack to cool completely.

4 Chill the tartlets. Whip the cream until it is just holding its shape. Place in a pastry bag fitted with a star tip. Pipe rosettes of cream on top of the tartlets. Decorate with chocolate curls and dust with unsweetened cocoa.

1 Sift the flour into a mixing bowl. Cut the butter into small pieces and rub in with your fingertips until the mixture resembles fine bread crumbs. Stir in the sugar. Add enough water to mix to a soft dough, then cover the bowl, and chill for 15 minutes.

cook's tip

The tartlets can be made up to 3 days ahead. Decorate on the day of serving, preferably no more than 4 hours in advance.

mixed fruit florentines

These classic cookies can be served with desserts, but they also make delightful petits fours. Serve at the end of a meal with coffee, or arrange in a shallow presentation box for an attractive gift.

Makes about 40

⅓ cup butter

½ cup superfine sugar

2 tbsp golden raisins or raisins

2 tbsp candied cherries, chopped

2 tbsp candied ginger, chopped

1 oz sunflower seeds

¾ cup slivered almonds

2 tbsp heavy cream

1 Lightly grease and flour 2 cookie sheets or line with baking parchment. Place the butter in a small pan and heat gently until melted. Add the sugar and stir until dissolved, then bring the mixture to a boil. Remove from the heat and stir in the golden raisins or raisins, cherries, ginger, sunflower seeds, and almonds. Mix well, then beat in the heavy cream.

2

3

2 Place small teaspoons of the fruit and nut mixture on to the prepared cookie sheet, allowing plenty of space for the mixture to spread. Bake in a preheated oven, 350°F, for 10–12 minutes, or until the cookies are light golden in color.

3 Remove from the oven and, while still hot, use a circular cookie cutter to pull in the edges to form a perfect circle. Let them cool and go crisp before removing from the cookie sheet.

4 Melt most of the chocolate and spread it on a sheet of baking parchment. When the chocolate is on the point of setting, place the cookies flat-side down on the chocolate and let the chocolate harden completely.

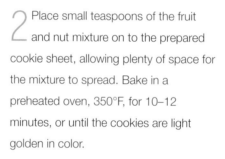

4

5 Cut around the florentines and remove from the parchment. Spread a little more chocolate on the already coated side of the florentines and use a fork to mark waves in the chocolate. Let set. Arrange the florentines on a plate (or in a presentation box for a gift) with alternate sides facing upward. Keep them cool.

refrigerator fudge

Chocolate, nuts, and dried fruit—the perfect combination—are all found in this simple-to-make fudge.

3

Makes about 25 pieces

9 oz dark chocolate

2 tbsp butter

4 tbsp evaporated milk

3 cups confectioners' sugar, sifted

½ cup coarse chopped hazelnuts

¼ cup golden raisins

3 Remove the bowl from the heat and gradually beat in the confectioners' sugar. Stir the hazelnuts and golden raisins into the mixture. Press the fudge into the prepared pan and level the top. Chill until firm.

4 Tip the fudge out on to a chopping board and cut into squares. Place in paper candy cases. Chill until required.

3

3

1 Lightly grease an 8-inch square cake pan.

2 Break the chocolate into pieces and place it in a bowl with the butter and evaporated milk. Set the bowl over a pan of gently simmering water and stir until the chocolate and butter have melted and the ingredients are well combined.

cook's tip

The fudge can be stored in an airtight container for up to 2 weeks.

variation

Vary the nuts used in this recipe; try making the fudge with almonds, brazil nuts, walnuts, or pecans.

quick chocolate vanilla fudge

This is the easiest fudge to make—for a really rich flavor, use a good dark chocolate with a high cocoa content, ideally at least 70 percent.

2

Makes 25-30 pieces

1 lb dark chocolate

½ cup unsalted butter

14 oz canned sweetened condensed milk

½ tsp vanilla extract

4

4

cook's tip

Store the fudge in an airtight container in a cool, dry place for up to 1 month. Do not freeze.

cook's tip

Do not use milk chocolate, because the results will be too sticky.

1 Lightly grease an 8-inch square cake pan.

2 Break the chocolate into pieces and place in a large pan with the butter and condensed milk.

3 Heat gently, stirring until the chocolate and butter melts and the mixture is smooth. Do not let boil.

4 Remove from the heat. Beat in the vanilla extract, then beat the mixture for a few minutes until thickened. Pour it into the prepared pan and level the top.

5 Chill the mixture in the refrigerator until firm.

6 Tip the fudge out on to a cutting board and cut into squares to serve.

variation

For chocolate peanut fudge, replace 4 tbsp of the butter with crunchy peanut butter.

spicy hot chocolate & hot orange toddy

A rich and soothing hot chocolate drink in the evening can be just what you need to help ease away the stresses of the day.

Serves 4

SPICY HOT CHOCOLATE

2½ cups milk

1 tsp ground mixed allspice

3½ oz dark chocolate

4 cinnamon sticks

½ cup heavy cream, lightly whipped

HOT ORANGE TODDY

2½ oz orange-flavored dark chocolate

2½ cups milk

3 tbsp rum

2 tbsp heavy cream

grated nutmeg

cook's tip

Using a cinnamon stick as a stirrer will give any hot chocolate drink a sweet, pungent flavor of cinnamon without overpowering the flavor of the chocolate.

2

3

5

1 To make the Spicy Hot Chocolate, pour the milk into a small pan. Sprinkle in the allspice.

2 Break the dark chocolate into squares and add to the milk. Heat the mixture over low heat until the milk is just boiling, stirring all the time to prevent the milk from burning on the bottom of the pan.

3 Place 2 cinnamon sticks in 2 cups and pour in the spicy hot chocolate. Top with the whipped heavy cream and serve.

4 To make the Hot Orange Toddy, break the orange-flavored dark chocolate into squares and then place in a small pan with the milk. Heat the mixture over low heat until just boiling, stirring constantly.

5 Remove the pan from the heat and stir in the rum. Pour into cups.

6 Pour the cream over the back of a spoon or swirl on to the top so that it sits on top of the hot chocolate. Sprinkle with grated nutmeg and serve at once.

chocolate milk shake & ice cream soda

These delicious chocolate drinks will make a chocoholic's relaxing summer day just perfect!

Serves 2

CHOCOLATE MILK SHAKE

2 cups ice-cold milk

3 tbsp drinking chocolate powder

3 scoops chocolate ice cream

unsweetened cocoa, to dust (optional)

ICE CREAM SODA

5 tbsp chocolate dessert sauce

soda water

2 scoops of chocolate ice cream

heavy cream, whipped

dark or milk chocolate, grated

3

5

6

4 Sprinkle a little unsweetened cocoa (if using) over the top of each drink and serve at once.

5 To make the Ice Cream Soda, divide the chocolate dessert sauce between 2 glasses. (You can use a ready-made chocolate dessert sauce, or the Hot Chocolate Sauce on page 215.)

6 Add a little soda water to each glass and stir to combine the sauce and soda water. Place a scoop of ice cream in each glass and then top up with more soda water.

7 Place a spoonful of whipped double cream on the top, if desired, then sprinkle the cream with a little grated dark or milk chocolate.

1 To make the Chocolate Milk Shake, place half of the ice-cold milk into a blender.

2 Add the drinking chocolate powder and 1 scoop of the chocolate ice cream. Blend until the mixture is frothy and well mixed. Stir in the remaining milk.

3 Place the remaining 2 scoops of chocolate ice cream in 2 serving glasses and carefully pour the chocolate milk over the ice cream.